A Heart of
KINDNESS

Wendy Comeau

In my opinion, life begins with kindness from
the heart and it ends with the people with the kindest hearts.

Wendy Comeau

FriesenPress

Suite 300 - 990 Fort St
Victoria, BC, V8V 3K2
Canada

www.friesenpress.com

ISBN
978-1-5255-1548-4 (Hardcover)
978-1-5255-1549-1 (Paperback)
978-1-5255-1550-7 (eBook)

1. BODY, MIND & SPIRIT, INSPIRATION & PERSONAL GROWTH

Distributed to the trade by The Ingram Book Company

A Gift For:

_____

From:

_____

Wendy Comeau

"Friendship is not about who you've known the longest.
It's about who walked into your life, said
"I'm here for you," and proved it."

—Unknown

Picture from the home of the Reddick-Desmond Garden, N.S.

Thank You for My Blessings: A Heart of Kindness

"Your mind is a garden, your thoughts are the seeds,
the harvest can either be flowers or weeds."
—William Wordsworth

"Where there's hope, there's life. It fills us with fresh courage and makes us strong again."
—Anne Frank

Table of Contents

A Heart of Kindness

Wendy Comeau

Dedication

This book is dedicated to my family, who has taught me that with life comes hope and new beginnings. I will always be grateful for the love, courage, wisdom, strength and kindness you have all provided me with on our journey. Thank you for a life of opportunities and challenges. Thank you for teaching me the most important lesson—that where there is life, there is hope for a new beginning, opportunities, and endless challenges. Thank you for letting me walk a journey of a lifetime with all of you. I have you in my heart, always.

Forever Grateful,
Your Daughter
Your Sister
Your Mother
Your Friend.

Wendy Comeau

"Kindness is the language which the deaf can hear and the blind can see."
—Mark Twain

Acknowledgements

To my husband, Robert,

I know that our love and faith has been tested beyond belief. Thank you for always holding me tight when I lost my words; for being my rock when all the rocks were gone; for being there when there were no words left to speak. But most of all, thank you for your lifetime of love and friendship. I will love you through eternity.

Love always,
—Wendy

To my daughter, Jennifer,

Thank you for your love, courage, strength, and friendship. When most children were planning a future, you were walking the unforgettable journey of a lifetime. I know we all found our different gifts and blessings through this journey, and you will always cherish these memories we shared. Thank you for realizing that no matter what happens in life, life is good.

Love always,
—Mommy

Friends,

I have learned gratitude from all of you; thank you for reaching out and handing me the lifeline to move forward and find that flicker of hope I needed for a new tomorrow. I was given a heart of kindness from the first to the last day of the journey with each person, and there were incredible gifts: a gift of love, a gift of kindness, a gift of friendship, a gift of faith, a gift of courage, a gift of strength, a gift of patience—and more than anything, a gift of hope for a new tomorrow. I have decided not to mention people by name; I do not want to leave anyone out. However, all of you know what you did on the journey of a lifetime we walked on, and I would like to thank each one of you. It is with your gifts and blessings that I could find my new day—my tomorrow. Thank you for your hearts of kindness.

Forever grateful,
—Wendy

"Kindness is more than deeds. It is an attitude, an expression, a look, a touch. It is anything that lifts another person."
—Plato

God's Minute

I've only just a minute,
Only sixty seconds in it.
Forced upon me, can't refuse it,
Didn't seek it, didn't choose it,
But it is up to me to use it.
I must suffer if I lose it,
Just a tiny little minute,
But eternity is in it.

—Dr. Benjamin E. Mays

Wendy Comeau

"Without deep reflection, one knows from daily life
that one exists for other people."
—Albert Einstein

Introduction

Reflection is always a good thing when we are trying to decide about our life, where we have been, where we are going, or where we want to go. Sometimes it takes a while to take that step, but when we do, everything seems to fall into place and make sense. This book is my first step back from a journey of a lifetime. This is the beginning of me healing and telling people that they too can heal a broken heart. It does not matter what event has taken place in your life, whether it is the loss of your job, a house, a pet, a marriage, a friend, a child, a mother, a father, a brother, a sister, or any event not mentioned in these pages— you can heal your broken heart.

The important thing to remember is that you can heal; you can find your hope for a new tomorrow. It may take you a little while to reflect and realize you need to ask for help or accept the lifeline from a good friend or a stranger that has been offered to you from a heart of kindness. Kindness matters most when it comes from your heart. A heart of kindness is the best thing we can offer to people who need to heal when they feel alone.

"Butterflies can't see their wings. They can't see how truly beautiful they are, but everyone else can. People are like that, as well."

—Unknown

It is important for you to realize that you are not broken—that the problem is not in your head—the problem is in your heart. Yes, your heart. And it can be healed. It was not until I looked deeper into my heart that I started to heal. I found questions I had been searching for that I needed answered. I had to reach deep within to be able move forward.

People need love in their hearts, but most importantly, they need hope in their hearts. Why, you might ask? Why? Because without love and hope, you cannot grow, and in my opinion, it is impossible to have the genuineness you need to have compassion for other people and care what happens to them. To want to stop and help anyone, you need to have a heart of kindness.

I looked for answers. I asked *why*. I could never find answers to the questions until the day I started asking myself the right questions, and I started searching for the information deep within myself, in my heart. I was not looking for anyone to blame. I just wanted to know why. I could not even get a good idea of what "why" looked like, and I realized I needed to stop asking myself that question.

I was told once that reflection was good for your heart, mind, and soul, and that upon deep contemplation of my life, I would be able to see and understand why and how events in my life unfolded the way they did. I could think back on the oneness and take my ego right out of the picture. This is good for your soul; it is good for you to reflect and feel the peace that one needs to have to live in a world of turmoil. To be able to reach deep within in your heart is to love yourself and a higher power. It is about leaving your ego behind and feeling that you are doing something wonderful to feed your soul.

This journey was not an easy one for me to walk with my family. By travelling with me through these pages and words, you may realize how difficult it was. Looking back, I would not have missed it for the world. It was a hard walk as a daughter, sister, mother, and friend. What I did not realize until a friend threw me a lifeline was that I still had my blessings. I received gifts from my family along the way that I could use, take with me, and carry in my heart forever: gifts from friends and strangers with a heart of kindness. No one could ever ask for anything more than the genuineness of a stranger when there is nowhere else to turn. It is my hope that with this opening prayer, "God's Minute," and the rest of the prayers, poems, quotes, and questions in this book that you come to see how I still had my blessings. My hope is that if you need to heal your heart, you can grab any lifeline that is available for you to hold onto, and you too can find your hope for a new tomorrow.

With hope for a new tomorrow,
—Wendy

Wendy Comeau

"The meaning of life is to find your gift. The purpose of life is to give it away."
—William Shakespeare

Gifts

Believe it or not, everyone we meet in our life leaves us with a gift. I have received lots of gifts from the people I have met—some were amazing, some were not so great; I can honestly say that I would have loved to re-gift some of them back. Think of all the gifts you received from people, good or bad. Just like a material gift, you can pass the gift on, or you can keep it and learn from it and still pass on the knowledge. I am going to share this gift I was left with from my family. For this, I will always be grateful.

Problems

I have learned that there are many problems in life, and it is how you look at the problem to resolve the issue that will make you a stronger person. It is about finding solutions.

Learning

I have learned that whatever you do in life has a lesson. You can learn about something new every day, no matter how old you are.

Giving
I have learned that when you give to someone else who may need something like food, clothes, or just to feel good and have a smile put on their face, it is the best feeling. It's like you just gave yourself a gift.

Dreams
I have learned to dream, because when you do, anything is possible. You can always believe in yourself and be happy when you dream.

Gratitude
I have learned to be thankful for a new day, as well as for the simple things, or all the little things in life. I have learned to always say "thank you."

Laughter
I have learned that if you can laugh, the world is a better place. You must be able to laugh, even in a tragedy, or you may never laugh again.

Love
I have learned that love is giving 100% from your heart to make someone else's life happier and easier in hard times.

A Perfect Day
The perfect day was putting a lifetime into one day to make a lasting memory for the family members left behind.

Friends
I have learned that you may only have one true friend in a lifetime, and you should never take friends for granted.

Family

I have always believed in my family. They are there for you to lean on, hold you and support you when the world seems harsh. The best gift you can receive in life is your family.

"Experience: the most brutal of teachers. But you learn,
my God do you learn."
—C.S. Lewis

Christopher wrote several poems the week before he
became ill.
I will share a few throughout the book.

I Believe

I believe in God.
I believe in family, because they are always there for me.
I believe in friends, because they make life interesting.
I believe in sports, because they give excitement.
I believe in animals, because their eyes always cheer me up.
I believe in peace, because it feels good to be safe.
I believe in education, because learning gives you
knowledge about the world.

—Christopher Comeau-D'Orsay

"There's a loneliness that only exists in one's mind.
The loneliest moment in someone's life is when they are
watching their whole world fall apart, and all they can do is
stare blankly."
—F. Scott Fitzgerald

I have gone through many different events in my life, but nothing as life-shattering as losing my family. That experience shook my world as I knew it, and everything changed. Sometimes I thought it was too painful to just keep putting one foot in front of the other. My second brother was murdered in 1989. My dad, who was my hero, died of cancer in September 2003. My son was a breath of fresh air; he died of a rare disease called Batten Disease CLN1 in November 2012. My mom was a lady who gave from her heart, and she died of cancer in December 2013. My oldest brother died of cancer in July 2014.

Now, you may be thinking, *how many mirrors did she break in this lifetime?* I am sharing this part of my life with you not for pity, but for understanding. I believe there are many lessons to be learnt from our family—every death of a family member has left me with a gift—yes, a positive gift of family. What a gift it is to be a part of a family, to love, to understand, to be patient, to dream, to hope, to grow, to work together to resolve issues that can cause undue stress.

Everyone has a story, and every family has problems. I realize that you never know what curveball life will throw your way. I thought I had lost all my blessings in life; I had not. I received many blessings on this journey of a lifetime. You have a choice:

you can choose to take the lifeline that someone is kind enough to offer and work towards finding your hope for that new tomorrow. My friends, and even strangers, gave me the hope to look forward to a new day, a new tomorrow. The flicker of hope that was left in my heart when the last family member died turned into hope; it began with me finding the positives in such a heartbreaking experience. It is not a journey I would have chosen to take, but it is a journey I would never have missed. My gifts, my blessings, were my family and the gratitude I have for each one of them, which I will always carry in my heart.

I learned to put a lifetime into one day to be able to fulfill the wishes of some of my family. I learned to be grateful for the simple things life offered: the sunrise, the sunset, the rain, the wind, the snow, the walks on the beach, the quietness. But most of all, I learned to listen—*really* listen—to the words and what people don't say.

"I am thankful for my struggle, because without it
I wouldn't have stumbled across my strength."
—Alex Elle

Even though I had all the support of my husband, daughter, friends, and strangers, I am most grateful for my faith, and for having the strength and courage to pray for the hope I needed in my life for a tomorrow. I believed that a new day would help me find my faith in a higher-power God, and that I would find a tomorrow worth living and move forward from my experiences. I will always treasure my gift of family.

In my opinion, education and knowledge is the key to teaching people how to move forward in the world. What I think creates change is sharing your lived experiences with people. It is more empowering for people to know that they too can live through any challenge life offers them, and that when they are ready, they too can find their opportunities in that little flicker of hope.

When I started this journey of a lifetime, I was a daughter, a sister, a mother, a wife, and a friend. The further I went, the more I felt I lost my identity. I lost my parents; I felt I was no one's daughter. I lost my brothers; I was no one's sister. I had no family, and most of all, I lost my child. There is not even a word that you can find to define the loss of a child.

The point I am trying to make is that I realized I needed words or a label to define who I was. I was using words to define who I was. I had always had a title of some sort, but that was gone with my family. How I connected to life was disappearing. I felt there was nothing left to offer. I could not find my strength to get out of bed. I would eventually see that titles in life do not define who we are. It is what is in our heart—in my case, a heart that was lost and empty. I felt I could not endure another loss. I could not find the courage, strength, love, faith, or hope to endure one more day. However, I was wrong. I could, and I did.

I thought it was important to feed my heart, mind and soul, because if you do not feed yourself spiritually, you will wither up and die before your time. Your light will lose its flicker. I had a heart of gold when it came to helping others. I did not need recognition for it. What I wanted was to help people realize that kindness matters most when it comes from the heart. A heart of kindness is the best thing we can offer to people when they feel broken and alone. When people are alone and feel they cannot find the courage and the strength to continue to a new day, all they may need is to have someone smile and say hello to them to want to carry on and move forward into a better tomorrow.

"The truth is, you don't know what is going to happen tomorrow. Life is a crazy ride, and nothing is guaranteed."
—Eminem

People do not realize that their gift of a "hello" in the morning or a smile may make a difference for someone. They do not realize they could be that one person who could help someone. Sometimes it can be devastating to carry on living out a simple day. But a smile and a hello could be the reason someone continues to find the hope and courage to wake up and take that step into tomorrow. Can you imagine the power you have with just a smile and a hello? Leave home every day remembering people need a heart of kindness today.

I thought I'd lost all the blessings in my life until one day I realized my blessings were my challenges I would have to endure hard life challenges to learn the real meaning of life— to learn why I would need to get up, wipe my tears, and continue to live and find new meaning in my broken heart, which had been left behind. *A heart of kindness began within me.* I would have to find the kindness within to love myself and to heal from the inside out. I had a choice to stay in the world of unhappiness, or to change and have the courage to work on the things that caused the unhappiness. It all begins with change—the little bit of flickering light that was left behind to help me move forward with hope, peace, love, and a vision that tomorrow could possibly be a better day.

Wendy Comeau

"I believe that at any given moment, you have the power
to say: This is not how the story is going to end."
—Christine Mason-Miller

I have looked at my life as chapters in a book. I am a firm
believer that when one chapter comes to an end, another
chapter will begin. Sometimes you just have no idea how each
part of the chapter will begin or end, or how life will take you
through the chapters, until you have a book. I have written my
book and started another chapter in my life.

I grew up with my mom, my dad, and three brothers. My
dad was in the armed forces, and we travelled a lot. We lived
in every province in Canada except two, and we also lived
in Europe. We moved more than anyone could believe in
our lifetime.

My dad came home one day, and my mom was standing
on a chair hanging the last pair of curtains in the house when
my father said, "Do not bother to hang the curtains; we were
just posted to another base." I could not believe it—we had
not even been there a week. When you have a parent in the
army, everyone is in the army . . . You do live a different sort
of life, compared to civilian life. I think this experience as a
child prepared me for my life as an adult. You learn life skills,
and most of all, you learn that life can change in a matter
of seconds. My routine had greatly changed, but I can honestly say I will always remember the days with my parents
and brothers on the army base during the military parades as
another chapter in a book of memories I have completed.

I went on to marry and have a family of my own. I was blessed with two beautiful children: a daughter, Jennifer, and a son ten years later, named Christopher. Christopher used to say, "Life is good." I believe that children can teach us more than we know about life. For a child, Christopher had much insight into the world. He told me one day that "life is hard, but not impossible." I thought, *what ten-year-old says that?* I knew exactly what he meant. He was losing his sight, and he took the attitude that life without his sight would be hard, but not impossible.

The rare disease Christopher was diagnosed with was Batten Disease CLN1, and it would eventually shut down every part of his brain, and then death would be upon us. It is a cruel disease that takes away any hope of the life you may have had for your child and brings you to the raw reality of death.

"Being a warrior is not about the act of fighting.
It's about being so prepared to face a challenge and
believing so strongly in a cause that you are fighting for that
you refuse to quit."
—Richard Machowicz

A Warrior's Challenge

I would like to share a little bit about Batten Disease. I realize many people have not even heard of this disease. It affects 2 to 4 of every 100,000 live births in the United States. It also affects people worldwide. Because Batten Disease is genetic, it often strikes more than one family member. It is inherited when both parents carry one defective gene; the children must inherit two copies of the defective gene to have the disease—one from each parent. In those cases, a child has a 25% chance of being affected with Batten Disease, and a 50% chance of being a carrier (National Institute of Neurological Disorders and Strokes).

Batten Disease is a neurodegenerative brain disease that primarily affects children between infancy and school age. There are more than ten forms of the disease, there is no cure, and it is always fatal. It causes seizures, visual impairment/blindness, personality changes, dementia, and the loss of motor skills and the ability to walk, talk, and communicate. In 2002, when he was fifteen, Christopher was diagnosed with the disease. Until then, we had never heard of it. It was a tragedy to hear there was no cure, but as parents, we walked an unforgettable journey of a lifetime with our son, learning and fighting for him as we walked.

I believe our government and health care system need to do more for people with rare diseases in Canada and around the world. Unfortunately, our dream was not realized for Christopher; on November 13, 2012, he lost his battle with Batten Disease CLN1, but as his family, we still fight the war on Batten and other rare diseases in hopes that someday there will be a cure that could be a reality for someone else's child. Research into treatments for "orphan diseases" is limited by their lack of frequency. Patients are few, and so little research funds are devoted to finding cures. This disease is mostly supported by donations and fundraisers for research. I am hoping we can bring more awareness to people and educate them about rare diseases and the lack of treatment options.

"Become one of the rare people who don't know how to quit."
—Robin Sharma

Research on Batten Disease has made progress since Christopher's diagnosis in November 2002; however, there are still more questions than answers. For more information on Batten Disease, you can visit www.bdrsa.org.

Christopher Comeau-D'Orsay received the Queen Elizabeth II Diamond Jubilee Medal posthumously on March 13, 2013, at the RCMP Headquarters in Newmarket, Ontario, Canada. He received this medal for his contribution to his community and country. The efforts to obtain access to the medication for the treatment of Christopher's rare neurological disease had highlighted problems that those suffering from rare diseases were having. After an investigation by the Ontario Ombudsman's office, a report, "From Hope to Despair," out-lined the problems. The Inherited Metabolic Diseases (IMD) Program had become so degraded by administrative neglect that it had become moribund: useless. The very program designed to help victims like Christopher and provide the kind of specialized expertise needed to administer health for such rare and destructive conditions had wasted away because of bureaucratic infighting and lack of commitment (see page 2 of "From Hope to Despair," 2005).

This investigation inspired another investigation into the lack of screening for rare diseases in newborns: "The Right to Be Impatient." While reviewing thousands of pages of docu-mentation obtained from the Ministry of Health and Long-Term Care during the Comeau-D'Orsay investigation, the

Special Ombudsman Response Team (SORT) investigators discovered an e-mail from one senior bureaucrat to another that read:

[There is] the potential for [the ombudsman's investigation into the funding for drugs to combat Batten Disease] to get into the whole IMD [Inherited Metabolic Diseases] program, including the screening issue, where . . . there have been 5 deaths from MCAD and Coroner's opinions voiced.

The direct result was the introduction of a program to screen newborns for a variety of genic diseases so treatment could begin as early as possible (Ombudsman Ontario, 2006).

"Tears are the safety valve of the heart when too much pressure is laid on it."
–Albert Smith

When Christopher received his diagnoses, he did not say, "Why me?" He did not cry, he did not pity himself. He said he had his faith, and sometimes it seemed stronger then everyone else's. We had so many questions that we were unable to get answers to. We had no idea what we would do or what this would mean in the days ahead—all we really knew was that death was upon us. That was the only sure thing.

Christopher knew what to do; he told us exactly what he wanted, and we took our son's words and wishes and kept them in our hearts and minds every time we had to make a major decision. These were hard to make for a mother and father; however, in the end, it was Christopher's love and faith that guided us, and it made this journey of a lifetime so much easier.

One morning, when Christopher woke up, he called me into his room and said, "Mommy, do you have a cold, or are you crying?" I said I had a cold. He was very perceptive and now blind, so I could go with the cold story.

He said, "Do not cry, because even though I am dying, I have the best mommy, daddy, sister, and family in the world, and I will always be with you no matter where I am in this universe or beyond." He also said, "Remember this, Mommy—life is good."

I stopped crying that day, and I poured all the love, hope, and dreams of a lifetime into as many days, weeks, and years that I could get. We worked hard to remember to make the best memories for the loved ones left behind. I started to look at life in a different way. I started to believe that my memories were going to be important to me, and that every moment mattered. We were going to savour the birthdays, Christmases, Easters, the Thanksgivings—we were going to cherish the moments more than we could ever imagine possible.

"No act of kindness, no matter how small, is ever wasted."
—Aesop

We needed to have the love in our hearts to endure a trip we did not want to ever take with Christopher—it was a trip we had to take. It was not our choice, and it was not an option we would have liked, if given a choice. We were on this trip because we loved him. He was our son, our child, and we were going on this journey with him. We were walking it with him, because every moment was a memory, and every decision was a memory; everything we did was an accomplishment, every conversation was precious, and every laugh, every tear, everything was about success. If we could end the day with laughter, it was a good day. Christopher taught me to laugh in tragedy. "Mommy, if you do not laugh at this, you may never laugh again," he said. Now, looking back and reflecting on his life, he left me with the gift of laughter, and so much more—he was a brave heart. He was the reason that kept me moving forward. He was my gift from God. Christopher brought us the gift of peace at the end of the day.

"The source of all abundance is not outside you.
It is a part of who you are."
—Eckhart Tolle

We are proud of the journey of a lifetime that we could walk with him. He had a lot of insight into life and death, and his legacy will live on in our hearts forever: "Life is good." Little did we know how much our children could teach us about life.

I believe life will always be a challenge, and there are many obstacles in the way. It is what you do with the life you were given that makes you different. It is how you face your challenges that sets you apart and makes you unique from everyone else. For instance, it has been almost five years since Christopher has died. We miss him, and nothing will ever be the same again, but he has left us with just three words: "Life is good."

Christopher was my inspiration for going back to school and becoming a Social Service Worker and Certified Coach Practitioner, advocating for people who cannot advocate for themselves. He was my inspiration for my business, Unique Creative Ornaments. I created it to help people in the community that needed a hand up, and to give back to the community. Christopher believed in the community in which we lived. Christopher believed that people deserved as many chances as it took in life to get things right. Our family believed in him, and he made our world a better place—he made us better people. I believe Christopher telling us "Life is good" makes it easier to get out of bed every day and make a difference for someone else who truly needs a hand up. I believe that life does change, and that life-changing moments are all about empowerment and meeting the challenges and goals we need to set for ourselves. I do believe our children teach us many lessons in life, and sometimes it is not a question of whether the glass is half full or half empty—sometimes it is more important that you realize that at least you have a glass. It has taken me a lifetime to learn that life is a journey; there is not a destination. Life is continual; it can be happy, devastating, or life-changing. Life is good, and life goes on—this is what I like to say is the beginning of another chapter I must write in my book of life.

The Cricket and the Spider

This journal is about a cricket and a spider and how they became friends. They are special in their own ways, even though they don't know it.

The cricket was not happy, because people told him he was ugly. He wanted to be like the butterfly, so he could be beautiful. One day the cricket went to the dragonfly, who told him that it was not worth wishing for, because it wouldn't happen. The cricket met the spider, who felt that he was uglier than the cricket. The spider's web broke, so he had to fix it—which he did to the cricket's music.

The spider and the cricket were special, but had to find out how. The things I should remember that make me special are: I'm friendly, nice, I get along with everybody, and I have a great sense of humour. Everybody is special in their own way, even though they might not know it.

—Christopher Comeau-D'Orsay

"I wanted to become a woman who overcomes obstacles by tackling them in faith, instead of tiptoeing around them in fear."
—Renee Swope

My Chance

I had to take this chance; I could feel I was losing me. I needed to believe in me again. It was tough to be strong; it was tough to tell myself "I am strong"; it was tough to tell people that I found my strength; it was tough to say the words "I believe in me," but I said them anyway. I needed to believe I would survive the harsh reality of death—sometimes I thought life was so much harder than death could ever be. That meant I would really have to work harder on my self-talk to go on. I had no other choice. I had to be strong so I could eventually find my courage to put that one foot in front of the other to appreciate another day in life. It was almost like I was playing a game with myself. If I said it, I would begin to believe it. I could start to imagine my days without my family; it was not easy. It was a process, it was difficult, and most days it was challenging, to say the least. Eventually, the concept began to work, and as the days passed, I could see myself smiling more. I could see I cared.

Creativity played a part in me moving forward. I thought if I could possibly use my imagination and feed myself positive words that eventually my words would make a difference in how I felt and what other people said to me. I have never understood people's intentions when it came to the words they used. Sometimes people would ask questions or make comments that were ridiculous, and I would be thinking, *what made them ask that question, or what the heck are they thinking? Really?* I did try hard to give people the benefit of the doubt, but sometimes it became clear that they just needed a book on etiquette, because they had no idea how their questions and comments made me feel. It was a case, sometimes, of them having their own agenda.

I soon discovered that if I could imagine myself doing things I enjoyed, I would do them. I imagined myself going for long walks, and I went for long walks. I imagined myself swimming in the pool every morning, and I went swimming. These were my little steps back to who I was.

I know I was lost—there is no question about it—but how was I ever going to find Wendy again?

"No matter how bad your heart is broken,
the world does not stop for grief."
-Faaraz Kazi

I had to be creative. I had to spend time talking to myself to keep moving forward into another day. With the kindness of my husband, my daughter, my friends, and strangers that came and went every day, it was becoming easier. I was starting to heal; I could find myself changing. Every day I could appreciate the walks on the beach, the sunset, the laughter of other people. Slowly, I was beginning to heal my heart. It felt like it had crumbled into a million pieces a few short months ago. But now it was showing signs of change, of growth. I was moving forward. I was learning to live without my family—I was growing into a new me. I was shedding my cocoon and turning into the butterfly I was afraid I could never become.

I was not afraid anymore. I was not hurting; the pain was not as deep. Yes, I still missed my family, I still thought about all the bountiful blessings and gifts I had been given and missed in my life, but it was not consuming me. I discovered I could move forward, that I had my blessings of faith, strength, courage, hope, and love for the moment. I did not need to plan for a future; I did not need to do anything but think about the moment I was in, because I could not look that far forward. I could only plan for a moment at a time.

I found the poem "A Minute" (included at the beginning of this chapter) in my mom's prayer book. She had so many prayers and pictures in the book it was like I was discovering another part of her that I had forgotten. It gave me comfort to sit down and go through her prayer book and discover all that she carried in it. There were pictures and names and dates of all her family members, the dates they were born and the dates they died, marriage dates, who married whom and how many children they had, as well as the children's names. I was amazed at all the information. I was also amazed that she had been given that book when she was sixteen and had carried it and kept it updated until her death. I knew my mom loved and believed in her family as much as I did. I did not realize she was keeping a diary within her prayer book of all the important events that had occurred in her life. For this is one of the many blessings my mom left me with, and for that I am grateful. She left me with this last thought: she said, "I do not want you to cry tears for me; remember all the little things we did, and remember to never to give up on love or the people who don't know the value of having God's Minute. Remember God's Minute—'I've only just a minute. Only sixty seconds in it. Forced upon me, can't refuse it, didn't seek it, didn't choose it, but it is up to me to use it. I must suffer if I lose it, just a tiny little minute, but eternity is in it'" (Dr. Benjamin E. Mays).

"Kind words can be short and easy to speak,
but their echoes are truly endless."
—Mother Teresa

My mom recited the poem to me and said, "No tears. Thank you for understanding, thank you for your love, hope and kindness, remember to keep the kindness you have shared with your family in your heart." These are all the little things she wanted me to know. Growing up, I never did find out what my mom considered big things. I thank you, Mom, for all the moments we shared in all the days we had. Thank you for all the wonderful gifts you have left me with, and thank you for being my mom.

The only thing that becomes important is the appreciation for the things not completed in your life, and the things you will miss when that person is gone: their laugh, their jokes, the singing. For me, it was the excitement of picking up the phone and telling my mom I was going on a trip, or that my dream of writing my first book was finally realized. It was singing my brother's favourite song to him ("Two Sparrows and a Hurricane" by Tanya Tucker) and never being able to sing another song after that day. I felt sometimes that every blessing and gift I was given in life was slowly being taken away. I would have to look deeper to find them as I continued the journey.

"This is my simple religion. There is no need for temples;
no need for complicated philosophy. Our own brain,
our own heart is our temple; the philosophy is kindness."
—Dalai Lama

My dad and I could talk forever; we could find a subject and make up stories forever. I had never thought about death or my dad dying before until I received the phone call saying he was sick and he was not going to make it. I had spoken to him for two and a half hours before the phone rang to say he was not going to make it. We were laughing and talking and he was having a conversation about my life. My dad said to me, "Do you remember when . . . ?" Looking back now, it feels like we talked about all the things he wanted me to remember about him, me, and us.

I said to him, "Yes, Dad, I will always remember when."

It was not until much later that I could reflect and have time to be quiet in the moment to understand that my dad was getting me to remember all the good times we shared. He ended our conversation with, "I love you; you are the best."

I would like to say every family member left me with a message, a sentence, a song, a word, or words of hope for the future. I am grateful I could have that last telephone conversation with my dad and sing my brother's favourite song. Those things, and the wisdom of my mother, are the gifts and blessings I received from them. I will carry them in my heart and reach for each gift as I need it in life. Thank you for all the hearts of kindness.

When We Plant a Seed

We Plant a Seed

...“When we bury the ‘seed,’ our faith needs to step in to remind us it takes time for new things to grow. As we continue to tend the idea/seed, we use our imagination to envision it growing and bearing fruit. We must be willing to let the seed have time and the room it needs to grow. Patience, persistence, and focus are important. Imagine life is a garden. What would you like to grow? A great job or business? A happy relationship? Children? Special goals and dreams? Planting idea seeds can start the process. Your action and energy will do the rest.” Marta Davidovich Ockuly (2017). JoyofQuotes.com.

A Heart of Kindness

"Once you begin to acknowledge random acts of kindness, both the ones you have received and the ones you have given, you can no longer believe that what you do does not matter."
—Dawna Markova

Awareness became my friend. I became aware of my actions, my feelings, and how I was filling my life with things to do and not taking on the real challenges I needed to fix within myself. I kept myself busy and filled my days, weeks, and years to avoid the pain of dealing with my grief and losses—until one day, a friend threw me a lifeline and told me I could talk to someone and they could help me with the pain. I thought, *how could anyone ever understand my thoughts, my feelings, my life, and my empty, broken heart that had nothing left to give?*

Awareness allows you to take the first step towards change. It is through awareness of your feelings that you start to accept the things that have happened in your life. I almost felt like my life was a movie I was watching, and that the things that had happened were not really happening. I was starting to see that I was not the person I had been before my family members all died. I became aware that I had changed. I was changing; I was becoming a sad, lonely person without my blessing or the gifts that had been so bountiful in my life just a few short years ago.

Acceptance was creeping into my life: this is the part that I came to understand as change; this was the seed my friend had planted when she threw me the lifeline that day. All she said was, "I know someone that you could talk to." That was her gift to me. Looking back, I am positive she had no idea what a gift she had given me. I did not realize I needed it until she had spoken her words of kindness to me, and for that I am grateful. After a short time, I remember how empowering those words were that she spoke that day. "I *could* talk to someone" became "Yes, I *can* talk to someone." That was the positive that came out of a short conversation. "I can talk to someone" meant I had a choice—I could change how I felt. I could fix how I was feeling. The words left me with the feeling of *Yes, I can, I can do this. I can change how I feel, I can change my thoughts, I can be me again. Something positive can come out of all the heartbreak I am feeling now because I can talk to someone. I can change how I feel about what I have been through.*

"You can love someone so much . . . But you can never love
people as much as you can miss them."
—John Green

In just a few short days, my friend had planted a seed. It
helped me to accept the circumstances I found myself in. It
helped me walk through the door of growth toward change—
change for the future, because I was never ever going
to be able to change the past. I could not go backward in
time and have what I so desired the most back. I could go
forward, I could walk through the door of growth and change
my thoughts and look forward to new beginnings. When you
reflect on life, it is an evolving door of change; nothing stays
the same. Things change every single day. Unless it is a major
life change, we do not stop and realize this.

For those of you that are reading this book and have children, you may go to bed, wake up, and then your child speaks
their first words or takes their first steps. They are growing
and changing in the world around us. How can that be? One
day they are walking, the next they are peddling their bikes
down the street, then they are off to jobs, college or univer-
sity, becoming doctors, lawyers, or anything they dreamed up
in their imaginations. We as parents had no idea they were
changing, growing and evolving so fast. Sometimes we just
don't recognize it unless we are looking for it—unless we are
standing still.

Before you can walk through that door of change, you must
be able and willing to start the process to make a difference
in your life. We can all reflect on each precious moment we

are given with our families. Change is good for us—it is hard sometimes, but it can be a very good thing for us. Sometimes it is hard because we are afraid of the unknown. The fact is that we have no control over what change will bring for us: it could be an adventure, and it could be positive, but if you do not like the unknown, change can be difficult. For me, I learned I could not alter the past, but I could look forward to the new changes in my life— a new tomorrow.

"If you change the way you look at things, the things
you look at change."
—Dr. Wayne Dyer

I now look at change as growth—a chance to challenge myself. It is not a good thing when the world around us is evolving and we stay in our comfort zone, because we are afraid to grow or afraid to see our children grow and evolve. Whether it is something small or a life-changing event, we can challenge ourselves to change what we do not like. After all, we get to write our own life story—it is our book to write.

"You are what you are and you are where you are because of what has gone into your mind. You change what you are and you change where you are by changing what goes into your mind."
—Zig Ziglar

Looking Through My Window at Life

The first year after everyone died, it felt like I was looking through a window watching everyone live their life. My husband, Robert, had a job—he had a life, and he had somewhere to go every single day. He had people to talk with, he had conversations, he could get away and forget about the terrible tragedies we had all been through as a family. Yes, I get the fact that someone had to pay the bills and put a roof over our head—that is not the point. My point is that he had a life after Christopher died, such as it was. His work was an extension of his family; he had people who helped him get through the days, months, and years just by him showing up every day at his job. He had that security of being able to move forward. He had a focus—he went to work and worked hard; he had an opportunity to do a job he loved with people he respected and people that respected him. It is hard to feel left behind and feel that the only thing you had left was a window to look out and watch every other person living their life. At the end of the day, all that you had to show for your life was a window with people going about their lives. It was not jealously I felt; it was the longing for what was important to me. It felt like I was missing an extension of myself.

I realized that I was programmed into the times of the day when Christopher needed to be turned or given medicine. I realized Robert was also programmed into turns and medication duty and he was getting up at night. Our home we loved so much with all the great memories had slowly turned into a place I did not want to be anymore. I fought hard to have a life after Christopher and the rest of my family members died. I went to Toronto to meet Robert for lunch, dinner, and shopping—every moment I could steal with him away from the house, I took. Somehow, that did not fill the void of my family. I needed something. I thought, *I cannot live in this house and not do anything while Robert is at work*. I was trying to pick up the pieces of my life and move forward. I was trying to find a place I belonged in life after my career as a mom, a daughter, a sister, and a wife had ended abruptly. There was no one left in the house to talk to or call.

"You can't just assume that everything will always be the same, because things change—especially people."
—Wilson Kanadi

The place felt like a lonely shopping mall when all the lights are turned off at the end of the day. I never heard so much quiet in one place. I am sharing this part of the story with you so you do not feel that I did not have any challenges or that it was easy to come back from where I had ended up after my family died. There are so many other things that happened in-between the pages that I cannot begin to even put on paper.

We had more trials and tribulations after Christopher died, my mom died, and my brother died. While I was in the process of selling my mom's house and packing it up and moving forward, I received a call from my daughter to say that the water softener had exploded and 100,000 litres of water went into our home and destroyed everything downstairs. Luckily, Jennifer and her now-husband had managed to salvage some of Christopher's mementos that I had packed before leaving for my trip. I had packed my mom's house to close that chapter of my life.

Sometimes it felt like I had a constant black cloud over my head; it felt like nothing ever stopped. I do not know if other people had these challenges in their life, but my life I felt like the challenges were never going to end. I didn't know if I would ever take the "hard hat" off again. This is an expression from a wise lady I met who offered up this analogy to me. She said, "Put the hard hat on and tie it tight, and do not take it off until the clouds are gone and the storm is over." I thought,

Wow, okay, what an analogy that was, because that is what I had to do to get through the difficult time in my life. Things did not stop after Christopher died for almost five years.

"Life isn't about finding yourself.
Life is about creating yourself."
—George Bernard Shaw

I would like to say that I am a stronger person for what I have gone through in my life. I do believe more now than ever that my challenges always made me stronger. There are opportunities that appeared that would never have appeared in the moment if I did not have these life challenges. I know this now, and I am grateful for every challenge I have endured. It has given me the opportunity to live in the moment, be in the moment, and stay in the moment. I do not ever have to plan for anything again. I appreciate the opportunities that come out of each moment in the time I have lived. After reflecting on my life, after all the trials and tribulations we went through as a family, parents, and a married couple, I think our priorities were in the right place.

I had to go through my own personal journey so I could grow from it and come to appreciate that life happens; you cannot ever plan it. When you least expect it, life will always throw you a curve ball and you need to know how to catch it, to grab the opportunity and run with the ball. If you miss the ball or drop the ball, you will always have another opportunity. This is called life. Now I know what it means to live in the moment in "God's Minute." To change, I had to believe in myself. I had to tell myself, "Yes, you can. You can do this." I had to have a talk with myself to encourage myself to believe in what I was doing. I had to instil a belief back into myself. I could not let doubt creep in. I had to stay positive. I had to believe in me; I had to do this for me. I owed it to myself first and foremost— this was the only way I was going to survive the healing process. I needed to believe in the lifeline that my friend had thrown me and I had to believe that there would be a new day, a new tomorrow for me. There was a future for me somewhere in this world. I had to believe in my higher power God. I had to find my courage, my faith, my hope. I had to believe in things I could not understand to be able to heal the heart that was broken into so many pieces. With this belief, I started slowly moving forward.

Healing a broken heart and understanding that you can heal this took me through so many different doors of life. For me, this book it is about resilience, and realizing that I would never give up on any of my family members, and that I was not going to be giving up on me. I was not given a choice—there were no other choices to be had. I had to be strong. I had to endure this process to heal. I had a flicker of hope left in my heart to love myself and move beyond the pain I was feeling. This broken heart was not going to stay broken. This heart was going to heal. This heart would find the strength—there could be no other way to heal.

Wendy Comeau

"Friendship is the only cement that will ever hold the
world together."
—Woodrow T. Wilson

I would have to learn on this journey of a heart of kindness
how to be kind to myself and give myself the courage to allow
myself the kindness I would need to heal. Because no one
else could do it for me. I needed to do it for myself.

I needed to gather all the tools and knowledge I had in my
heart, mind, and soul to move forward to heal myself. This
would turn out to be my appreciation of an experience and a
journey of a lifetime after I came to realize that a heart of kindness had to begin within myself. I had to have the courage to
love myself, to find acceptance and understanding to reflect on
what my heart, body, and soul had gone through. I had to give
myself permission to grieve for each of my family members,
and I had to learn to say to myself that these feelings of hope-
lessness would pass and that my self-talk were my words of
opportunities—they had to be positive words. There was no
room in my life for self-doubt; not if I was going to help myself
to a better place—a future with hope, love, courage, strength,
faith, change, and the unknown. A future without an empty
heart, a feeling I could picture with love, hope, and kindness
in my heart and the people around me. How great would that
be to be able to truly remember every family member without
a pool of tears? I believed I could, so I did.

My family, friends, and the strangers I met on this journey
made it possible for me to heal. I am finding the process you
go through to heal from a loss in your life—whether it is a

loss of a family member, a job, a pet, a marriage etc.—is something you need to go through to grieve, and it cannot be skipped, because you cannot heal unless you go through it. You must appreciate the experience of what you lost and you must realize what you have been through has changed the way you think and look at the world—it is what I call gathering the knowledge to examine the three important things I needed to move forward from where I was in this moment of uncertainty.

"Try and be a rainbow in someone's cloud."
—Maya Angelou

I needed to give myself the kindness to heal. I needed to feed myself with kind words when I felt alone, and I needed to understand and realize that I still had my blessings and gifts in life that I had before each family member died. I had to work hard at finding the opportunities in all the life challenges I had endured in such a short time to be able to keep breathing and moving forward from the beginning to the end of each day. Sometimes those days seemed so long by myself; sometimes the days felt like weeks. Life as I knew it would never be the same. I had to work through what happened and put it into the right perspective to understand the lessons and what opportunities I could find moving forward into the future.

I have always said that everyone has a story and everyone has life challenges; it is how we handle them that sets us apart and makes us the unique individuals we are in this vast world we live in. We can all walk the same journey and everyone will be affected in a different way. My husband, my daughter, and I have all experienced it in a different way. Robert experienced his journey with me as a father, husband, son in-law and brother in-law, and I experienced the same journey as a mother, daughter, sister, friend, and I came away with different experience and insight. Our daughter Jennifer experienced her journey as a sister, granddaughter, and niece, and she did not have the same experience as my husband or myself. I think it is important to realize that no two people see the same situation the same way. Our feelings, our thoughts, and our brains all process things differently.

46

"There are two educations. One should teach us how
to make a living and the other how to live."
—John Adams

I am strong, and I am not going to give up hope. I am going to embrace this experience as a learning tool, and I am going to learn how to heal and move forward into the future, because some day someone may need to have the knowledge of my experience and want to know how I managed to change the challenges of despair into the opportunities of a heart of kindness.

Someone may just ask me that question someday, and I will be able to speak up and tell them, or they may read about it in this book. Either way, they will get the help they need and their questions will be answered.

"Gratitude is not only the greatest of virtues, but the parent of all the others."
—Marcus Tullius Cicero

Sometimes people have no idea what you went through. That is okay, because everyone's journey in life is different. What everyone could do is reflect on the journey they have been on and never judge anyone else for the journey they have chosen for themselves. I do believe that we must find our own solutions to our challenges and our own opportunities. Never compare the journeys we walked to the journeys of another person. I believe somewhere deep inside our heart, mind, and soul is where you will find the uniqueness of who you are. If you take the time to meditate and reflect, you will find peace; you will find your blessings that you carry inside your own heart.

These blessings are your uniqueness, your individuality—no one else has your gifts or talents. They are there for you to reach for to be used when life has sent you a challenge and you need to find the solutions. You have your beliefs, your strengths, your courage, your patience, your love, your hope, your faith your charity to do good, your smile, your kindness. This is what you reach for when you look deep down inside yourself. This is your lifeline to use when you need one. Reach for it. Never give up on yourself or on hope. You will be surprised at how strong you are when you are faced with life-changing moments for yourself or someone you love. Hold on and do not ever give up, because no matter how tired you are, all those things you have inside of you will sustain you for another moment, another day, until you find your flicker of hope, your strength to face the challenges in your life, and to give you peace of mind, heal your heart, and find the kindness that you lost in the moment of all the turmoil in the world.

Wendy Comeau

"If the only prayer you said was thank you, that would
be enough."
—Meister Eckhart

Words

Watch your Thoughts

Watch your thoughts,
for they become words.

Watch your words,
for they become actions.

Watch your actions,
for they become habits.

Watch your habits,
for they become character.

Watch your character,
for it becomes your destiny.

—Frank Outlaw

A Heart of Kindness

"Dreams and dedication are a powerful combination."
—William Longgood

People ask what inspires me. My answer is that people inspire me—their stories inspire me, what they think and why they think the way they do inspires me. People's lives and challenges inspire me. How they got to be where they are, how they managed to get through some of life's most difficult moments inspires me. When you listen, really listen, to what people say, it inspires me to help make a difference in their lives or someone else's life in the future.

People that are homeless ask me why I am like I am. At first, I did not understand that question. They wanted to know why I cared when no one else seemed to, and why I used kind words. I was talking to a person who lived on the street, and he wanted to know why I cared if he ate? Why? I cared if he had a place to live. I explained to him that everyone has a story, everyone has a road to walk, and sometimes the road can be devastating. He agreed that it could. I spent time talking with people who were homeless or almost homeless and I listened to hear the messages they gave. Sometimes you may hear it in one word or sometimes in many—sometimes even in tears.

What are words, after all? Can you imagine our life without them? Just think about it for a second. Did you know that our choice of words can make a huge difference to our lives, and to many other people's lives? Did you know it is common for us to use negative words that change our attitudes, thoughts, or what other people think of us? The solution for this is to change our negative words to positive words. To change our thoughts, we must change our words so we will think and believe in a more positive way. It is all about what we believe. If you tell yourself negative things, you believe nothing but negative things, and nothing good comes out of anything negative.

Words matter to me because people are hurt—sometimes devastated—by the word or words we choose to speak to them. They may never heal or be able to move forward in life because of a word or sentence someone chose to use on them. I have listened to people tell me that they would have rather been slapped or punched in the face, because they could heal from that pain, but they will never heal from what someone has said to them out of anger or jealously. We can choose our words better; we can choose to be kinder and more understanding to people. It does not take any more effort on our part; we only need to watch our words.

"What we are today comes from our thoughts of yesterday,
and our present thoughts build our life of tomorrow:
Our life is the creation of our mind."
—Buddha

Be positive. Say kind things to people and help them understand that the world is not an unkind place to live. Sometimes people live a whole lifetime with a label or words that have made them feel like they are less valuable than they are. People have been classified with words, and it has been a fight for them to overcome this—most of the time they could not fight the system. We are crippling people with words and labels, and it starts with our children. The words that are used become their legacy in life, and they will either fight back or give up hope. In my opinion, it is easier to use kind words and be genuine to people so that they can heal from the inside out. People do not need to feel that they have less of a chance of happiness in life because of the words we choose to speak. This is not on the person suffering the outcome; it is on the person who chose to spit out the words. "Be sure to taste your words before you spit them out" (unknown).http://www.searchquotes.com

Power comes in many different forms; you have the power to take control of your emotions, you have the power to make changes, and you have the power to change your words from the negative words to the positive words so that you can say, "Yes I can, yes I will, it is up to me, I can change what I do not like." When you change your words, you change your thoughts. Think about that statement for a few minutes—it is all about what you tell yourself.

Wendy Comeau

"Clear your mind of can't."
—Samuel Johnson.

You can. If you think you can't, you won't, and if you think you can, you will. Remember, your words are your thoughts—they are what you believe about yourself, so chose your words wisely. You have the power to do this. It is all up to you.

Words have power. One word or phrase may bring a world of self-hatred into our life, or one word or one phrase can make us love our life and the world around us. Show people that kindness matters most when it comes from the heart. Kindness does not cost you anything.

"It takes but one positive thought when given a chance
to survive and thrive to overpower an entire army
of negative thoughts."
—Robert H. Schuller

Take the time and make it a daily practice to say something kind to someone every day. You never know if your words will be the words that someone needed to hear to get through their day or if they are the last words that someone will hear. Start by making a list of positive words and add it to your vocabulary. Take the time to add new positive words to your list every day. Make sure you use the words on yourself and other people.

Then challenge yourself. Add a couple more of your own positive words every day to the list, and before long you will be thinking and feeling differently. The words we choose inspire us to change. Words stay in our memory for a lifetime; our words are our expressions of our emotions, and we take them everywhere with us. The first word spoken by our children brings pride and joy and leaves an impact forever.

There are more than 6,500 spoken languages, in the world. However, about 2,000 of those languages have fewer than 1,000 speakers. The most popular language in the world is Mandarin Chinese. There are 1,213,000,000 people in the world who speak that language. Chinese tops the list of most popular world languages, with over one billion speakers. English trails in third place, with 335 million speakers. This data represents first-language speakers ("Most widely spoken languages in the word," n.d.).

Words can give us self-confidence, words can tear us down, words can bring the world together, or they can separate everyone. Words can teach us compassion, and they can send a message to make people feel like they are sitting on top of the world. Our words are how we determine what we think about ourselves and the world around us. Our words are our decisions. Our words express our wants, desires, and dreams.

Listen to our children and how they speak, and you will see and hear clearly what words mean to them. You will also see how they interpret the words people use on them. Words are the book of life we write for ourselves, and our children choose to use positive ones and choose them wisely. It's up to you; the possibilities are endless for what you write on the pages of your book of life. Make sure it is a book you can be proud of—after all, in the end, you want to be the one that can enjoy reading it after it is written.

"The greatest weapon against stress is our ability to choose one thought over another."
—William James

My life—and I can only assume yours, as well—is filled with challenges that make it very difficult to be positive sometimes. I am constantly striving to see the positive in every aspect of my life. But it is not always easy. It doesn't always come naturally for me, and sometimes it's a lot of work. Even when things are difficult, I know that being positive and striving to make the best of whatever situation I am in does make even the most challenging situations easier to bear. I also believe a positive attitude makes the challenges easier to resolve. Your choices in how you handle them seem more abundant than if you take a negative approach.

When you are thinking negative thoughts, it appears you cannot find one solution to the challenges. The opportunities you would have had if you had a positive attitude go unnoticed, and you are unable to find opportunities. Teaching myself that positivity is a choice has been one of the greatest things I've ever done for myself; when you can focus on being positive, your world opens to more opportunities than you can dream of and you have an endless supply. Keep your life free of negative thoughts, words, and people if you want to live a positive and happy life. Limit negative or toxic people who don't encourage your happiness. I do not mean to get rid of people in your life who may be going through a hard time; I mean if you have a friend who is negative about life or cannot find the joy in anything in life and is constantly putting down everyone and sees nothing good in people. Toxic people are draining, so limit them in your life.

Look for the positives in your life. In every challenge in life there is something positive, so find at least one positive opportunity in one life challenge. If you begin to look at your life challenges as opportunities, you will start to feel more positive about your life. In every challenge in life in every situation, in every negative person you meet there is always an opportunity to find something good. It may not be easy to find the good or kindness, but if you look hard enough and reflect, I know you can find at least one positive aspect in your challenges or in the person who was negative to you.

"Think twice before you speak, because your words
and influence will plant the seed of either success
or failure in the mind of another."
—Napoleon Hill

Sometimes you may have to look harder to find the good. Making sure to think and stay positive means that you must believe in yourself, so you could give yourself a positive talk every single day—sometimes several times a day. You could reinforce your thoughts and behaviours; you could believe in you. You cannot let negativity flow into your thoughts. It is all about the power of positive thinking—you believe what you think. Share your thoughts on positive thinking with others, and always be nice to people, even when they are unkind to you. Say thank you often, give someone who is having a bad moment in their day a hug, listen to what people are saying, listen to understand. Really listen. You will be surprised at what you hear.

These ten words are especially powerful, and present us with an opportunity to understand more about ourselves and how we use the words:

"The most selfish one-letter word: 'I.' Avoid it.

The most satisfying two-letter word: 'We.' Use it.

The most poisonous three-letter word: 'Ego.' Kill it.

The most used four-letter word: 'Love.' Value it.

The most pleasing five-letter word: 'Smile.' Keep it.

The fastest spreading six-letter word: 'Rumour.' Ignore it.

The hardest working seven-letter word: 'Success.' Achieve it.

The most enviable eight-letter word: 'Jealously.' Distance it.

The most powerful nine-letter word: 'Knowledge.' Acquire it.

The most essential ten-letter word: 'Confidence.' Trust it."

—Arise Training and Research Centre

"Be yourself—not the idea of what you think somebody else's idea of yourself should be."
—Henry David Thoreau

Who Am I Really?

Looking for answers or asking the right questions: which is better, in your opinion? Can anyone ever find the answer to a "why" question? I have spent the better part of my life asking why. Then a light came on in my head when I overheard a mom in a shopping mall say to her young child, "If you ask me why one more time today, I am going to leave you on this chair to think about all the why questions you have. I will continue to shop and have fun by myself."

For me, the last several years have been why questions. *Why did this happen? Why did that happen? Why am I so unlucky?* The list can go on and look like Santa's naughty or nice list or like a mess of wasted paper on the floor. The key word here is "wasted." A "pity me" trip is a waste of time, energy, and your life that is not helpful to you or anyone around you. Recently, I discovered that you cannot answer the question "why" without having "why" come back to you. I was looking for answers instead of asking questions.

What does your gut tell you? What does your inner voice say? Those are the questions you need to be asking. Those are the only questions that need to be answered. Ask the right questions to focus and go in the right direction from the beginning to get your questions answered. My question then became, "Who am I really?" Who am I? Not who I want to be, not who I pretended to be, not who others expected me to be, not who I was yesterday, last week, last year, or a decade ago . . . who am I really?" When you take everything away and let yourself answer the question—heart, mind, and soul—you will find yourself becoming empowered and letting go of the assumptions. You will be able to find the answers to "Who I am really?" You will be able to find your abilities, accomplishments, attitudes, dreams, likes, dislikes, passions, blessings, and so much more. There are a lot of questions you can really answer in your life if you leave "why" out of the equation. Ask the right question: "Who am I?" Not what others perceive me to be; for me, I discovered, life has a purpose. I am a survivor, life is a journey, life is continual, life does not have a destination, and life is good.

"Attitude is a little thing that makes a big difference."
—Winston Churchill

The Man in the Glass

When you get what you want in your struggle for self,
And the world makes you king for a day,
Just go to a mirror and look at yourself,
And see what the man has to say.

For it isn't your father, mother or wife,
Whose judgment upon you must pass,
The fellow whose verdict counts most in your life,
Is the one staring back from the glass.

Some people might think you're a straight-shoot-in' chum,
And call you a wonderful guy,
But the man in the glass says you're only a bum,
If you can't look him straight in the eye.

He's the fellow to please, never mind all the rest,
For he's with you clear up to the end.
And you passed your most dangerous, difficult test,
If the guy in the glass is your friend.

You may fool the whole world down the pathway of years,
And get pats on the back as you pass,

Wendy Comeau

But your final reward will be heartaches and tears,
If you cheated the man in the glass.

—Unknown

"If you look for the bad, you will find it. If you look for the good, you will find it. We always have a choice between two realities: the positive and the negative. The reality we invest our energy in is the one in which we exist."
—Yehuda Berg

Do not let negativity flow into your heart, mind, or soul. Do not let people play mind games or try to manipulate you into feeling guilty or letting you be the solution for their issues. I feel that I have learned a lot on this journey. It was not just an awakening; it was a spiritual journey that tested me way beyond what I could imagine I could ever endure in a lifetime, let alone a few short years. Did I feel that I could not endure any more disappointments and the suffering of people dying all around me? I sure did.

I also came to realize that people can be vicious. I met several on my journey, and I quickly learned they had their own agenda. They had their biases and their own pain. They went out of their way to be cruel and unkind. Okay, every-one you meet in life is not going to like you or get along with you—I agree with that statement 100%. However, why in God's name do they need to be so cruel, mean-spirited, and cause so much grief to people who already have the weight of the world on their shoulders? I will tell you why: they enjoy inflicting pain on people who appear to be weak, who appear to be suffering, and appear to be living and holding on by a thread. Why? I think this because I experienced it several times over the past few years while I was trying to help myself. I had these vicious people make me question who I am, if I was truthful, if I was genuine. I was. I discovered they were not any of these themselves. They had their own unresolved problems, and I just happened to be the person they could use to make themselves feel better. Sometimes, I have discovered in life, it is much easier to blame people for your own mistakes or misfortunes than to stand up and own your own shit and take responsibility for it. That is why I chose to use the word "vicious"—there is no other word I could find that describes people that would do that to another human being, especially people who think they have the power over a situation or an event that you may find yourself in.

"When someone is vicious toward you they are giving you a glimpse of the pain they carry in themselves. Viciousness is suffering."
—Bryant McGill

I was going to leave this part of my journey out of the book. However, I thought it would be a good life lesson for the reader and a bigger lesson for the person or persons who caused me the grief to read about it in the book. It is my hope that the person who needs a lifeline will grab it. Make the changes in your life you need for your future happiness. You will have so much more to offer people in your life. You will find the genuineness that you are often describing to others that you have seemed to misplace on your own journey through life.

It all comes down to an opportunity for a learning experience. It was a challenge for me, like everything else was in life. I asked myself to put things in the right perspective and I finally found a box and filed them into things you want to know about in life in case you need to teach this to your children. My daughter, who is insightful about people and life, told me I had to learn about this, as it was not in the lessons I taught her or her brother. My parents did not bother to teach me about vicious people, because they probably thought there were not that many in the world. I believe they may have been right.

Vicious people are people that have their own pain that they have never dealt with. They do not know how to reach for a lifeline that someone has offered them, or they believe they do not need one. Keep believing that you don't need to fix your heart, mind, and soul and eventually you will run out of people who will stand by you and support you when you are playing havoc with their lives. The quote at the top of this page and in this paragraph is for you to read over and over until it resonates with you and you get the help you so deserve. "When someone is vicious toward you they are giving you a glimpse of the pain they carry in themselves. Viciousness is suffering".
—Bryant McGill

To the people who hurt me: You were a challenge for me, but out of that challenge came many opportunities. I learned to deal with people like you, and I learned that because you acted the way you did. It was not on me, it was on you; it was your pain that you carry in your own heart. It is your suffering, not mine, therefore I did not need to add it to my list of misfortunes.

"Life is a shipwreck, but we must not forget to sing in
the lifeboats."
—Voltaire

I also learned that usually the cruellest people can have kind hearts; you just need to look a little bit deeper to find their heart of kindness. My final opportunity or gift I received from this challenge in my life was recognizing when someone needs a lifeline, throw them one. They may surprise you and grab it and make use of it. It is with a heart of kindness that I hope you will take the lifeline that I am extending to you and use it to become the happy, caring person I know you would like to be.

I am grateful for the lesson on viciousness and the many challenges and opportunities I have received from it. I have learned that when all else fails you, faith and hope in a higher power will get you through, one moment, one hour, and one day at a time. The "God's Minute" prayer I came across tucked into my mom's prayer book was meant specifically for me, to help me realize that I do not need to look so far into the future that I cannot see myself. I can take a minute and build from there. I will decide when I can consider the future again, and right now I think I like planning things in the moment. I have a much deeper appreciation for living in the moment and appreciating every sunrise, every sunset, every breath I breathe. I thank my higher power God for the kindness he has shown me and the love and kindness I will carry for every-thing I have seen and experienced with friends, family, and strangers. Sometimes it is very hard to be thankful for our challenges and harder to realize that you can take a lesson and an opportunity from everything you endure in life.

The only thing you realize upon deep reflection, meditation, and insight is that you have the resilience to get through another day and bring knowledge with you into tomorrow because you still have your faith. With faith, I could believe things were possible. I was always taught if you can breathe there is life, and with a living, breathing life, there is always hope. I still had the hope and the faith left to believe in my higher-power God. You can and will always be able to see a tomorrow. You just need to never give up on your higher power, whatever that may be for you.

"I could have missed the pain, but I'd have had to miss
the dance."
—Garth Brooks

Forgiveness

Do It Anyway

People are often unreasonable and self-centered.
Forgive them anyway.
If you are kind, people may accuse you of ulterior motives.
Be kind anyway.
If you are honest, people may cheat you.
Be honest anyway.
If you find happiness, people may be jealous.
Be happy anyway.
The good you do today may be forgotten tomorrow.
Do good anyway.
Give the world the best you have and it may never
be enough.
Give your best anyway.
For you see, in the end, it is between you and God.
It was never between you and them anyway.

—Mother Teresa

Wendy Comeau

"Hope sees the invisible, feels the intangible, and achieves
the impossible."
—Helen Keller

I am going to venture out and say that most people have
a spiritual belief in something in the universe that is unknown
to them. A higher power, a spiritual belief, that there is something out in the universe that they cannot see or understand.
Whatever you believe, find time to nurture your spirituality in
your life. Be kind to yourself, reflect on your day or minutes
in the day, meditate, and/or concentrate on one word or a
phrase to keep you grounded. See beyond someone's unkind
words or behaviour. Maybe if you give them a thank you or a
kind word back they will stop and realize how you made them
feel and pay your act of kindness forward. I look back on my
journey now with much more insight, and I can say people do
not realize that kindness is free. People will always remember
that you were kind to them when they needed kindness most
in their life, and they eventually will pay it forward when they
realize it is much easier in life to be kind-hearted.

In my opinion, it is important for you to forgive people who
have been unkind to you. If there is any lesson in life that you
need to understand, it is that it is important to forgive a person
who has treated you or a family member with malice. My
brother was murdered, and I never forgave the person who
took him out of our life. I could not understand how someone
could be so selfish and cruel to another human being. Looking
back, I think I could have used forgiveness on that person
who took my brother's life for her own selfish purpose. I really

could have told her I forgave her for taking my brother from a family that loved him and leaving my parents' hearts hurting for a lifetime. I could have said, "I forgive you." Because I chose not to say those words to that person, I carried with me that person's baggage, and I found it harder to live my life. I felt the emptiness; I felt the birthdays, the holidays, and the pain of my parents' loss with every special anniversary that went by. I could have said a prayer, written a forgiveness letter, tore it up and thrown it in the garbage or burned it. I could have healed myself and taken that pain out of my heart.

"Forgiving does not erase the bitter past. A healed memory is not a deleted memory. Instead, forgiving what we cannot forget creates a new way to remember. We change the memory of our past into a hope for our future."
—Lewis B. Smedes

My brother did not deserve to have his life taken away by someone so jealous of him. The only one she wanted to hurt was his family. We loved him and he was a person who could see the good in everyone—even people that he knew he could not trust. He would say, "Give people a chance. They might surprise you. You will never know if they will take the chance if you don't offer it." Sometimes I would think, *Yes, how will you know if you don't offer up that chance?* I do appreciate the fact that he had insight into the world and the people around him, even though he was just a few short years younger than me. He was a genuine person who really believed that if someone needed something and it was his last dollar in his pocket they could have it, because obviously if they did not need it they would not have bothered to ask. He cared about people, and he always trusted that people would do the right thing. Sometimes I used to think that is what got him killed in the first place. He trusted people too much. What I know now is that he would never have had it any other way. He told me he believed in people, and if you believe like he did, I know he would have thought everything would be okay. People have a choice; they can change if they take that chance. He loved life, and I know he lived his life the way he died. Now I know he took a chance and he believed in someone; he was willing to die for what he believed. He believed in giving people a chance, he believed in never giving up on people or hope, he believed that people get as many chances as it takes, because we were always taught as children to never give up, and to never give up on hope. People will and can change, and people will always surprise you. Thank you, Chris, for your gifts and blessings. You will never be forgotten.

"Forgiveness has nothing to do with absolving a criminal of his crime. It has everything to do with relieving oneself of the burden of being a victim—letting go of the pain and trans-forming oneself from victim to survivor."
-C.R. Strahan

My Brother, My Friend

Only God knows the life we saw
And the times we shared,
The many things we accomplished,
And the many things we dared!

The one thing I could count on
Was you by my side.
You were always more than willing
To go for a ride.

But I let my guard down,
And our adventures came to an end.
Now you had time to think,
And some time to mend.

So smile when you remember
Our brief time together, and know that I love you,

My brother, forever.

—Unknown

"Forgiveness is a virtue of the brave."
—Indira Gandhi

The challenge for me was not giving people another chance—it was forgiveness. Forgiveness, I have learnt, was not forgiving the person for the deed of harming you or a loved one. Forgiveness is important for your own wellbeing. Forgiveness helps you heal and move forward into another moment, hour, day, week, month, and year. Forgiveness helps you heal your own heart, mind and soul; you do not ever have to talk to the person to say the words, "I forgive you." You could write a forgiveness letter or say the words. It does not excuse the harm the person has caused you or your family. However, it allows you to have closure and move forward to begin healing. It makes things better for you. You are not harbouring negative thoughts or feelings within and causing yourself undue unhappiness. Forgiveness plants the seed for growth and healing. Forgiveness is accepting and moving forward—it is all about loving yourself and the world we live in. Healing does not ever mean that the damage did not exist; it means you do not let someone have the power to control your life or anyone who was hurt by the result of their actions. It allows you to take back your power and it allows you to stop being a victim. When you can stop and tell the story without having cried a pool full of tears, it means you have healed yourself by letting go of the anger, hurt, and betrayal you felt. You have healed. You are feeling safe now and can let go of the hurt.

Death or the loss of a relationship can leave you feeling angry and betrayed; however, if you can, forgive the person for leaving you in death or a physical relationship and appreciate what you had together and have gratitude for what you shared in the time you were together, life becomes a little bit easier to bear as each day passes; it allows you to always appreciate what you had in that moment in time. It allows you to remember all the good times you shared. It allows you to heal and move forward. Gratitude always allows you to stop and appreciate what you had in your life and it allows you to appreciate what you have now. In my opinion, loss brings you to the reality that nothing is ever guaranteed in life. You can only count on the moment you are in—the present of the here and now. It is difficult for me to plan a week, a month, or a year in my life.

"The world breaks everyone, and afterward, some are strong at the broken places."
—Ernest Hemingway

For the longest while, I did not keep a calendar or a date book for appointments. I could not understand why I became so disorganized when I was always an organized person who planned everything down to the last detail. I finally figured out one day that I could not plan for my future because I could not look at a calendar—it was too painful to look at the dates of birthdays missed, and it was even more painful to look at the dates of my family members' deaths. It amazes me when I reflect on my behaviours and the reasons I find myself doing the things that I do. I see how much I have grown; how much I appreciate what I have lost and what I have gone through to get to where I am in my life.

Life is fragile, and gratitude is what I feel for my family and friends I have lost, because without my losses, I do not think I would be the person I am today. Loss has taught me to appreciate the people in my life, and it has taught me to love and appreciate the little things. I understand completely my mom's words now: that the little things that happen in life are not important. The most important thing is to realize and have gratitude for all the things you do have.

The loss or the grief I have carried in my heart will never die; however, it will feel a little lighter and be a little kinder when I remember that I still have my blessings and I still have my gifts my family had provided me with just a few short years ago. Christopher said it exactly the right way to me that morning: "Mommy, I will not be here in body, but I will be in your heart forever," and that is one of my many blessings received on my journey of a lifetime, for which I am grateful. My family never left me. The love of family was important to me, and now, looking back, my parents planted that seed early in our life. The seeds that are nurtured when they are planted grow and become strong: your belief in family, love, and understanding grows a bond that is so deep in your heart nothing can grow but love.

"Keep love in your heart. A life without it is like
a sunless garden when the flowers are dead."
—Oscar Wilde

Love is what sustains you when you need the strength to be strong. Your love of self is what helps you to find the faith, hope, and compassion for other people and their journeys and stories.

I love to talk to people. I love to help people, and I love to hear their stories because I am always curious to find out how they overcome their life challenges and what made a difference to them. I am finding that talking and listening to people's stories is the key to helping people overcome their challenges and find new opportunities from what they have experienced. I cannot say it enough: you can move forward from any life adversities. You need to believe in you to over-come your challenges. It is important to have the love of self to find the strength to do it. You are worth it; you are worth every challenge you have endured in your life. Embrace your challenges, and embrace moving forward to your new oppor-tunities. With your journey, you became stronger than you can ever imagine yourself being. Embrace your strengths, because there is no room left in your heart for fear.

"Work like you don't need money, love like you've never been hurt, and dance like no one's watching."
—Unknown

Be Happy, Not Perfect

"There is no such thing as perfect. Where did the word come from? The perfect husband, the perfect job, the perfect house, the perfect marriage. We are all humans living in a human world. Most are nice, sincere, loving, even kind, but 'perfect' causes such unhappiness. Perfect is unreal, untouchable. Accept good, well done, and wonderful. Do your best to be your best. There is no such thing as perfect. Be happy, not perfect."

—Patricia Walter

"I can never decide whether my dreams are the result
of my thoughts, or my thoughts the result of my dreams."
—D.H. Lawrence

Do what makes you happy; show yourself the kindness you show to everyone else. Dream your dreams, follow your dreams, live your dreams—you have already been through some of the worst moments, days, weeks, and years. Things do get better. Life becomes a little softer and kinder, and you will find your passion for a new tomorrow. It is important to change and grow in a direction you never believed you could go. You know what you don't know that you know. Life is good, and you have a ton of wisdom to take with you into the universe and beyond.

I have learned and experienced what it takes to have a heart of kindness. I am not afraid to face the challenges that will come my way in the future. I know now that I must reach down within myself and find my heart of kindness and listen—just listen—to what my heart, mind and soul feel. Life is so much simpler in the moment. The door has closed on fear. I have opened my door to hope and all it can offer me. I know if I keep hope in my heart, I will never fear what another tomorrow will bring.

Life can be a struggle sometimes; it can be full of disappointments. However, it can be an adventure full of dreams, challenges, and opportunities for a positive life experience. The possibilities are endless when you decide to use your imagination and dream. Your future is yours; you hold all the possibilities in your hands, heart, mind, and soul. Everything is connected, and you can grow from life challenges with your imagination. Your opportunities are endless and rewarding. You are the one that holds your future in your own hands and you have the power to say, "Yes, I can. I am going to write my own story. This is not how the story is going to end. I hold the power to my own future, and I can and I will change what makes me unhappy." You have the power to control your emotions and thoughts.

Your life has a purpose. There is always something you can do to inspire people in this world. My purpose in life is seeing the value in people—listening to understand, never judging, always caring, believing and inspiring people to never give up hope. It is important for me to help people put value and hope back into their lives and help them see there can always be a new tomorrow.

"When people are determined, they can overcome anything."
—Nelson Mandela

It is important to me to inspire them to dream, to explore through caring, believing, and never judging themselves or others. Life is about treating yourself with kindness. It is important to allow yourself to find your passion. Your passion for life will then become your purpose, and your purpose will help you to continue to heal and to move forward. When you can find your passion in life, you will find that you have the strength for the impossible. Nothing will seem hard anymore, and you will discover that you have learned what life is all about. With your passion for life, you can live your dreams and find your inner peace. You have a deeper understanding for living in the moment. Things are easier and you can make the impossible happen—life is all about impossibilities. You will find the compassion for yourself and others, allowing you to keep putting one foot in front of the other as each day passes. You will be able to see yourself smiling more and finding new opportunities. You will never forget what you have lost. However, eventually, your focus changes a bit and you feel yourself healing; you can have compassion in your heart for the challenges of other people you meet along life's busy path. You find that you have a clear understanding of another person's misfortune, and you are willing to extend a helping hand, an ear to listen—really listen—to what they have been through.

You have changed how you look at life and what is important to you— everything is more important. You do not take anything for granted; you know what it means to be in this moment. It is hard to explain to people who have never had a loss why things have changed so much for you. They cannot wrap their minds around the fact that when you are faced with a loss it changes you; it changes your inner spirit, and you will never be that person you were again before the loss. It takes all the courage you have to realize that you are strong and you can recover. You need to trust and believe in you.

"Love, hope, fear, faith—these make humanity;
these are its sign and note and character."
—Robert Browning

Reflect and meditate to bring a deeper understanding of what you have been through and where you want to go to move forward into a whole new world. The knowledge you receive from reflection and meditation comes from deep within your heart, mind, and soul. This is where you find your true self, and your true answers to your own wellbeing. This is where you go for an understanding of who you are now, in this moment in time. This is how you heal. You bring awareness into your life for a kinder understanding of where you have been and where you want to go. It is about finding your inner peace, your spirit, your love for yourself, and a heart of kindness for you and everyone else in this universe. It is your connection to your inner spirit. It is a place for peace and a deeper understanding of the world and how you see yourself and how we are all connected. This is where you can find your higher power. It is where you can find the peace we are all searching for in this universe.

"The language of friendship is not words but meanings."
—Henry David Thoreau

I Pray

"In my life, I think I should pray for food and that my family and I avoid poverty. I am thankful that there is no war in our country, for my sense of humour and for my family. I pray that there will be no more suffering and war in other countries. I pray that there will be a cure for the sick and I pray that someday I will have my eyesight back. I pray there will be no more suffering in the world and nobody will live in pain."

—Christopher Comeau-D'Orsay

"Every great dream begins with a dreamer.
Always remember you have within you the strength,
the patience, and the passion to reach for the stars to
change the world."
—Harriet Tubman

Life-Changing Events

I graduated from the Social Service Worker program and I did my placement with an outreach centre. It was, I would say, an experience I will not forget for a very long time. To say it was "eye-opening" is an understatement. Homelessness, I believe it belongs to everyone in our community and our countries. It is the responsibility of everyone in our society to help make a difference and support community initiatives if possible.

It takes just one big financial hardship, and anyone could be in the same position. It is not about what happened or why the person is homeless and living in a shelter, on the street, or even on someone's couch. It is about stepping up and being part of the community and helping someone who needs the help. At the outreach centre, you wear many hats in the run of a day. You are a coffee maker, a breakfast server, a sandwich maker, a cleaner, a clothes sorter, a listener, a counsellor, a researcher, and a telephone answering machine. I mean, you can pick up the phone, answer it, put it down, and not even take a breath; it rings constantly from people calling with questions.

The facts may surprise you. What you hear people saying is that people with mental illness or an addiction want to live on the street. The homeless do not want to be on the street. Yes, we have participants with mental illness and addictions; however, we also have participants that are families—yes, families—who are on the street or close to being on the street because they are the working poor. They are people who have lost their jobs, run out of employment insurance, and cannot luck into getting a job. They are also the disabled. They are moms, dads, brothers, sisters, uncles, aunts, and yes, even our elderly population. It is an epidemic; they are not all what people assume homeless people are. The outreach centre is open five days a week from 8:00 to 3:00. They have a van that runs seven days a week and serves over 160+ people a shift. The van provides support, from sandwiches, clothes, hygiene products, blankets, groceries, baby needs, harm-reduction supplies, and counselling, as well as linking people to community partners that could possibly be beneficial.

A Heart of Kindness

"You must be the change you wish to see in the world."
—Gandhi

It is heartbreaking to see people in this city who cannot afford the rent, or if they pay the rent, they cannot afford the heat, gas, food, or other necessities of life. Every person you help is a success story; if they can find shelter for the night, food, dry clothes, and a hot cup of tea or coffee, they have had a successful day. Therefore, I continue to volunteer with other people in this city to help solve the issue of homelessness.

What can you do to help? You can drop a food item in the food bank box at the grocery store when you shop. You can volunteer at a shelter near your home, or you can make sandwiches and drop them off there or donate your gently used in-season clothing. You can make a hot meal, a dessert, or any food item and donate it to help an out-of-the-cold program in your neighbourhood. Our churches are full on a cold night. It is time for everyone to get involved. It is everyone's problem, in my opinion, and I realize that's worth exactly what you paid for it—nothing—but I just wanted to give it anyway. Open your hearts and do an act of kindness; donate your time, buy a food item, or simply donate to an outreach centre and help feed someone who needs your act of kindness.

In our hidden community, I have always wondered: who gets to decide if you are good enough? Who has that power over another human being? I have reflected to the point where my head feels like it is going to explode. I have come across so many different scenarios over the last few years in my own life, as well as in the lives of so many other people.

Let's say that people fall on hard times, and you are talking about the circumstances of homelessness, mental illness, and the senior population to people who do not appear to have these problems. How can people say that anyone chooses to be homeless or want to live on the street? I have come to the realization that people come to this conclusion to make themselves feel better so they do not have to justify doing anything about the situation or contribute to helping find a solution for the people in this world who need a hand up. I have heard all the arguments I can stand from people.

"No one is useless in this world who lightens the burdens of another."
—Charles Dickens

Who is going to pay these bills? Who is going to pay for shelter, food, clothing, and affordable housing? Who is going to pay for the people coming to this country from war-torn abusive countries? Who is picking up the bill? But wait— when you ask, "What is your ethnic background?" you get a response like, "I am from India," "I am from Germany," "I am from France," "I am from England," "I am from China," "I am from Russia," and the list goes on and on like a never-ending river. I rest my case. We are all from somewhere, and we all had help to get to where we are today. Our parents gave us a hand up, if we were lucky enough to have our parents help us, or we were lucky enough to have jobs, student loans, and make it through to the next paycheque by the skin of our teeth.

Everyone has a story about hard times, and you can some-times look back on life and laugh about it. But what about our homeless population? I know people do not choose to live on the street. I am going to say it again: everyone has a story and everyone has experienced hard times. Kindness is not much to ask of people. Open your minds to new possibilities and open your hearts, and this could help clean up our streets and find solutions for everyone who is homeless or almost homeless in this rich country in which we live. We need to stop overlooking the painful reality of the hungry men, women, and children living on our streets. We need to stop making excuses for not doing what needs to get done. If we have budgets for everything else in this country, we have money to feed the homeless or almost homeless in our countries. Stop blaming and shaming a population that has no power, and stop telling people they are not good enough to have a roof over their head. This does not do anything but make it easier for people to come up with excuses to do absolutely nothing.

A Heart of Kindness

"The most terrible poverty is loneliness and the feeling of being unloved."
—Mother Teresa

People have real-life struggles, and at the end of the day, all they really need is to find someone with a heart of kindness to help them find a solution to the challenges they find themselves in, in that moment. It is all about giving from your heart to make someone else's day a little brighter with a kind word or a hug— that may be all anyone may need: just a simple minute out of your day. Homeless people do not need to receive any more backlash from the community in which they live. They need understanding, they need help, they need food, clothes, compassion, and they need kindness. They do not need judgment; they do not need to be told that there is not enough room on the floor of a shelter when it is 25° or 30° below 0°. They don't need funding in a year, they do not need to be told, "We will see if we can help you in thirty days"—they need help now. Their lives matter. They are someone's mothers, fathers, sisters, aunts, uncles, grandfathers, grandmothers, and children—they are our soldiers that spent time in other countries fighting for our freedom and have fallen between the cracks. They are real people with real problems.

Look around the community in which you live. They are the hidden people who contributed and were hard-working people until they lost their jobs due to companies closing and moving to other countries or the end of the construction boom, or a life-changing event that caused them to give up total hope of moving forward. I have heard people say that before we can get the homeless shelter, we need to fix their addiction problems or their mental health issues. Has anyone ever considered the fact that the reason they have all the issues is because they are living on the street? The health issues could be a secondary problem, and if they get homes and people to help them adjust to having a nice warm place to live, food in the cupboard and some mental health education and care, that would make everyone more stable.

No one wants to live on the street. No one wants to see people go through the hurt and struggles that street people endure to survive one day to the next. In my opinion—and I have lots of opinions about homelessness and almost homelessness in our community—our cities, our provinces, and our countries need to clean up the streets and find small, attainable housing for the people who need the help. It is an epidemic that we cannot afford to be overlooking. Everyone in our community needs to realize that homelessness is everyone's problem—it is not a problem that happens to a small few. Working people are only one paycheque away from becoming homeless. The next time you say it could never happen to you, watch your words, because you can lose your job, you can lose your family, you can lose your house, you can lose your car, and then your dignity. You can be on the street, homeless.

A Heart of Kindness

"The way we do small things determines the way we
do everything."
—Robin Sharma

Give people their dignity back. Give them back their hope.
One person can make a difference, but a community working
together in a non-judgmental way can make a homeless
person feel that he/she is just as important as everyone
else in the society in which we live. It is all about being non-
judgmental and taking the action needed to help people move
forward into a new day. Please stop shaming a population
that is not guilty of anything but being unfortunate enough to
lose their families and their job.

Wendy Comeau

Good Enough

My child, beware of "good enough,"

It isn't made of sterling stuff;
It's something anyone can do,

It marks the many from the few.

The flaw which may escape the eye
And temporarily get by

Shall weaken underneath the strain and wreck

the ship, the car, or plane.

With "good enough" the car breaks down,

And one falls short of high renown.
My child, remember and be wise.

In "good enough" disaster lies.

With "good enough" the shirkers stop

In every factory and shop;
With "good enough," the failures rest and lose

The one who gives the best.

A Heart of Kindness

Who stops at "good enough" shall find success

has left them far behind.

For this is true of you and your stuff.
Only the best is "good enough."

—Unknown

"It's okay to not be perfect. It's okay to make mistakes.
It's okay to do something that you hadn't done, because
if we don't do those things, we never grow."
—Dawn Stanyon

Overcoming Mental Illness

The stigma of mental illness prevents people from seeking treatment because they are afraid of being judged and labelled with all the negative stereotypes. Therefore, many people and organizations are having mental illness awareness discussions to bring this into the open so that people can understand that it is like having surgery, cancer, or any other illness. It is a disease, and there is nothing to be ashamed of. In fact, according to *The Globe and Mail*, "the World Health Organization has identified stigma as a 'hidden burden' of mental illness and a major public health challenge" (Close & Stuart, 2013).

I think we are advanced in medicine enough to know that all kinds of things can cause a person to develop a mental illness, such as everyday life situations that may trigger a crisis, like financial problems, family problems, and things as simple as not getting a good grade. Depression is just one of the mental issues people are facing today. There are a lot of people suffering in silence because of what others think. Many in our community have mental disorders and do not go to anyone or seek counselling because they are worried about what people think. I think this is tragic for the society in which we live.

People should be able to trust and confide in other people without being judged. Understanding and kindness would be better than making the person feel that they are not worthy of help. Sometimes the biggest gift you can give is to listen without judgment and help someone take a step toward recovery. To judge someone and make them feel like they are less of a person because they have a mental illness shows a great deal of ignorance, and that is why education is so important. Mental illness can happen in anyone's family, and the more you know about a problem, the better equipped you are at helping to solve it. According to The Globe and Mail, there will always be challenges in mental illness "raising awareness and eliminating stereotypes, prejudices and harmful practices" (Close & Stuart 2013). It will take people and organizations speaking out to keep educating people. I think there should be programs in all schools, as it is important to bring awareness and stop the stereotyping and bullying.

"Often it's the deepest pain which empowers you to grow into your highest self."
—Karen Salmansohn

Mental illness is seen everywhere—on our streets, in jails, and in our homes and families. It is like a domino effect, and everyone needs to open their eyes to the fact that mental illness is a very big part of our community.

Government, social agencies, non-profit organizations, and people who volunteer will see more need for outreach programs if mental illness is not treated and the stigma can fester and continue to grow in our society. We cannot turn a blind eye and pretend this is not an illness.

"Putting people down does not make you a
powerful and strong person. It makes you a bully,
a coward, and eventually alone in life."
—Tess Calomino

I would like everyone to think that preconceived ideas about differences between races, cultures, religions, or anything that divides us could always be open to change. I think it is all about educating ourselves to the things we fear or what we don't know. Knowledge is power, and having the knowledge of people's differences gives you understanding and insight into why people feel the way they do and what caused them to feel that way. This opens a whole new world to helping people move forward with their life challenges and helps them to better find solutions that will help them resolve their issues with confidence.

It is easy for people to think they cannot do something because they fear other people judging them for whatever preconceived idea they may have about themselves. However, we could choose not to judge, and we could choose to inspire people who feel less valued in the world because society chose to label them, and now they are becoming self-conscious about what they have been told over the years that may not be true. It might be the opinion of someone who was in an authority position and had the power to use those words on people. But who gave the person labelling others and undervaluing them the right to do that? What makes them an authority? Does anyone realize that these people could have their own ideas about what they think people could or could not be? People do not need to go through life with labels. They need to be treated well and valued for who they are. Believing in people, showing them kindness, listening to them, understanding them, and making sure they feel heard and understood could go a lot further in life. It could have a more positive value than inflicting a label on someone's life to make them feel like they are less valued in the society in which we live. The most important thing people need is to know their life has value. Everyone is unique; they matter, and their future matters. No matter what challenges you endure, you are important to everyone in society.

We all value your uniqueness and your opinion matters to the world.

"Look for a way to lift somebody up, and if that's all you do, that's enough."
—Elizabeth Lesser

We need to inspire people to change the way they think and stop judging others. Everyone is different; there are no two people alike in this world. We are unique individuals, and we all have something to contribute. The world is waiting for us to discover our talents and stop labelling people, because that is hurting the population and causing people not to reach out and ask for the help they need. They know they are being judged long before their foot hits your office steps. Let's show some compassion, understanding, and kindness towards the people we work with, live with, and talk with in our community. Let's make this world a better, happier place to live.

Wendy Comeau

"Do not judge me by my success, judge me by how many times I fell and got back up again." —Nelson Mandela

Good Morning

Good morning, ladies and gentlemen and fellow students. Today I would like to talk about discrimination. Martin Luther King once said, "I dream of the day when people are judged not by the colour of their skin, but by the content of their character." For Martin Luther King, the discrimination and hatred of African Americans was not fair or proper, whether it was law or not. He led a movement that resulted in changing the way blacks were treated and not judged by just the colour of their skin.

"I dream of the day when I am judged not by my eyes, but for me. People see me as a blind boy first and treat me different than other guys. Often people avoid or ignore me, thinking I won't know they are there. They don't realize I see more than they think. People do not realize discriminating against others who are different makes life hard on everybody. People should not judge others because of how they look, but based on their heart."

—Christopher Comeau-D'Orsay

This poem was written by Christopher shortly before he became ill with Batten Disease CLN1.

Forgive Me

Forgive me, God, for my lack of faith. That I so easily give up. Forgive me, God, for not accepting you. That I sometimes can't accept what happens.

Forgive me, God, for my lack of patience. That I get angry so easily. Forgive me, God, for my lack of understanding. That I can be stronger than I have been. Amen.

—Christopher Comeau-D'Orsay

"If you fell down yesterday, stand up today." —H.G. Wells

Why You Don't Give Up

I do not give up on myself or life because I believe I have a purpose. I believe I could never give up on anyone who needed me. Life comes with many different challenges, and sometimes it can be harsh. However, if I give up, I would never know how the story was going to end. Even when I am most tired, I am not giving up. I need to know things will change when I least expect it; there is always a surprise around the next corner. You think things will never change, but they do. Never give up on your challenges, because you never know when things will change for you. If you miss one opportunity, another one will appear when you least expect it. This is the only positive thing I can say to you or to myself—you never know what moment you will find a new opportunity in.

You could be going through your own door of challenges when someone you meet might need you to hold the door open for them to walk through; it could be a new opportunity as you hold their door open and let them walk through. What I am trying to say is be kind to yourself and show kindness to a stranger, as you never know what kindness that stranger can show you. When you are going through your own life challenges, stop and look for the opportunities for a new beginning.

Showing people kindness is free. It does not cost you a dime—the only thing it may cost you is a few minutes of your time. Believe it or not, you may never get the time back that you spent being kind, but you will always feel the kindness within yourself by giving that few lost minutes to someone who needed it. Kindness is free, and the love you receive back from a kind deed is worth every bit of time you think you may have lost. You will put a smile on your heart, you will always feel your heart smiling, and the chances are that the person you showed an act of kindness to has a smiling heart and is feeling so much better. Always remember to be kind to yourself so it will be easier to be kind to others.

"Never allow someone to be your priority while allowing yourself to be their option."
—Mark Twain

Storms

It seemed that I was always driving through a storm—a rainstorm, snowstorm, or a storm of life. Sometimes I used to think my life would not be complete without a storm. Looking back now, I realize that all those storms had a purpose. I believe now that they were my life lessons testing my patience and endurance. Can you imagine having gone through life without being in a storm? How would that look for anyone? I am not sure if you would ever learn what your purpose in life was unless you had a few storms.

Sometimes I have had people ask me how it feels to have everything. I could not believe the question, let alone what I was hearing. *What?* Could you please say that again? When people look at another person's life, they do not ever see the real life of hardships and strife. They look at you as if you never had a care or struggle in the world; you just woke up one day and landed on this planet. How wrong they are to think like that about another human being. People are people, and just because you do not appear to have had storms in your life, it does not mean that the storms did not exist. Everyone has had them. Some may not have been tornados, but I can guarantee you that people have storms in their lives.

Some people try to grab their lifeline or their life jacket and hold on and float their way through the storms and make the best of the bad situations they are in by being positive and talking their way through it. They try to navigate and chalk it up to the little things in life . . . until another storm blows through. They take their storms as a learning experience and analyze it, asking questions such as, "What could I have done better?" "What did I learn from this experience?" "What will I not do again if I must go through the same kind of storm?" This is called the storm of life when you can take a lesson and learn from the experience you have just been through. You may not like the storm, or what you learned. You may never want to repeat the experience ever again. Nevertheless, it was your storm and your learning experience that got you through.

"What lies before us and what lies behind us are tiny matters compared to what lies within us."
—Ralph Waldo Emerson

It was your life lesson. Sometimes I wonder why people can look at you and think they see that you never knew a life challenge or what to do with a life challenge if you were to have one. My answer to that is they are only looking at you and judging you for their own purpose. They have their own agenda; they do not want to be your friend. They want to know you, they want to act like they had a life of hardship and that it is your fault that the hardships they endured left them without any opportunities in life.

I am not trying to be harsh about the storms people go through. We all handle them differently. Some people lament on the storms in their life; however, they never once stop and ask the questions of themselves they need answers to in order to learn how to move forward in life. They would rather stay stuck in the place they are in at this moment in time because it works for them; friends and family cater to their needs, they make people feel guilty for what they don't have in their life. However, they are quite willing to point out everything they think you have or what you may appear to have in your life. However, they cannot point out one positive thing in their own life or make a list of all the great life experiences they have had or one positive thing they are grateful for in their own lives. They see me as having everything in life, like someone dropped a bountiful supply of everything at my front door. This is not how things work. For every storm in your life, for every storm you walked, swam, or drove through, if you reflect on it, you will be able to find at least one positive thing.

People do not have everything in life. Life does not work like that. I have gratitude for what storms I have been through. I am thankful for them, because they made me the person I am today. I have an appreciation for life, not the things in my life. It is nice to be comfortable, but it is nicer to appreciate and feel thankful for all the little things that you have in your life.

My purpose for writing about the storms is that when you are walking, driving, and swimming through your storms, stop and appreciate what you have been through. Ask the questions of yourself that you need answers to. Move forward and be kind to yourself, and never let anyone tell you, "You have no idea what challenges are."

"Attitude is a little thing that makes a big difference."
—Winston Churchill

The person saying that is looking for you to feel sorry for them and guilt you into making their life easier so they do not have to deal with their own storms. They want you to feel guilty about where they have ended up in their life. They are not interested in finding a solution for the storms they are going through or have been through.

They want what they think you have, and they never, ever want to fix what is wrong. They want to tell you that you do not understand their story because you have not a clue on how the real-world works. In my opinion, people need kindness, love, and understanding in life. People can face their storms with the courage and strength to get through their challenges, and when they do, they will appreciate what they have been through.

My storms have changed me, death changed me, and there is no storm greater than death to challenge your life and how you begin to look at the tomorrows you have left on this earth. Be kind and be thankful for the minutes and moments in life. I am grateful for all the little things—there is nothing left that I need or want. To the people who think I do not know what a storm is—I know. I do not need to explain my storms to you. I can be kind and I can find some kindness in the storms I have been through. I can pass that kindness to people going through their own storms so they can ask their own questions and find the positives so they can move forward into new opportunities.

"A little thought and a little kindness are often worth
more than a great deal of money."
—John Ruskin

Happiness

Happiness is not found in money, and it is not found in material things. Think about it—why?

People who have everything in the world that their imagination can dream up are not necessarily happy; some are, but it is not the material things or money that makes people happy. Again, ask yourself: If you had all the money and material things you wanted in your struggle for life, would that really make you happy? No, I do not believe it would. Why? I believe if there is something missing in your life, you will never enjoy your wealth because you will be pining for what is really missing—something you cannot ever have, something totally impossible for you to attain. People that have wealth can be happy if they are lucky enough to have all their gifts and blessings to share their wealth. With the gifts and bountiful blessings comes gratefulness. Their life is fulfilled with all that they have, and they can be happy, not because they have wealth, but because they are grateful for what they already have—they do not want or need anything else, as their life is full. Their cup is overflowing. These people are truly grateful for what they have.

Now, getting back to the people who have everything and are not happy— they will never be happy unless they can obtain what is missing in their life, or unless they become grateful for what they have. In my opinion, all the money in the world will never buy the happiness people are searching for because that does not exist. The happiness you are searching for comes from within yourself. You provide your own happiness in life. Can you be happy? Yes, I believe you can if you can be grateful for what you have, and that does not mean you need 100 million dollars in the bank to be happy. It means you need to be thankful for what you already have in your life. You may be thankful for your crops growing in the fields after the long spring rains. You may be grateful to know that after all your hard work planting your crops, you will have a bountiful supply of hay to feed your animals through the long hard winter. The farmer is grateful—he is happy to know that he has a way to feed all his animals for another year, and his worries may be small until the next spring planting season.

"The grass is greener where you water it."
—Neil Barringham

Gratitude comes in many forms. Some people may be grateful to be able to put the food on the table and pay the bills for another month; they are happy their children have a home and food to eat and they can go to bed happy and start over again the next day to provide another meal for another day. This is what their happiness is all about—being grateful for what sustains you in life, which makes life happy for you, your family, and friends. It is all the little things you can provide for your loved ones. It is all about being grateful for what you can provide for each other. Kindness and gratitude are the keys to happiness.

So, if *you* can be happy, be happy. Do not ever wish for someone else's happiness. You never know if they are happy—they could have everything in the world and still not be happy. Remember, happiness comes from kindness and gratitude, not from worldly goods. In my opinion, happiness comes from within your soul, and you cannot be given happiness unless you have been given something you are grateful for. For myself, I am grateful for every breath I take, every sunrise, every sunset, for my walks on the beach with my husband, and for my bountiful gifts and blessings my family left me with. I am truly grateful and happy for my life.

"Too often we underestimate the power of a touch, a smile, a kind word, a listening ear, an honest compliment, or the smallest act of caring, all of which have the potential to turn a life around."
—Leo F. Buscaglia

What Can You Do for Kindness?

Ask yourself what small difference you can make in your life and someone else's life in the community in which you live. Can you say hello or good morning to a neighbour? Can you give a smile on your daily walk? Can you light up a room, put a smile on the face of someone who needs a kind word or a hug? Yes, you can—you can do all of this, and so much more without even thinking about it. We all could practice one little act of kindness every day. Saying thank you is an act of kindness. You could make your workplace happier by showing kindness and by saying thank you. There are endless possibilities you could come up with on your own. The important thing to remember is that kindness matters to people; they will remember the kindness that you showed to them. When you give kindness away, you will feel that you have given your own self a gift. It will put a smile on your face, and you will feel the gift of kindness within yourself. Our community, our schools, and our world need more kindness.

Everyone, I am sure, knows Christmas is not always about opening presents. It is about opening our hearts; it is about giving another person the hope of tomorrow, the strength for another day. If you can give anything to a person this Christmas, give the gift of a smile, a hug, or just a thank you. You will not believe how far that gift will reach into the future.

"Don't be disappointed if people refuse to help you. Remember the words of Einstein: I am thankful to all those who said 'no' to me. It's because of them I did it myself."
—Chocolate Socrates

About the Word "No"

Did you know that when you told someone "no" in life, that could be considered a good thing? Think of all the reasons you say "no" to people in your life. "No" can be considered an excuse for you not to do things in your life. "No" can be an excuse not to take a chance because you may have the fear of failing at what you do. "No" could mean so many different things to you, and "no" could be a benefit to you. If someone said the word "no" to you, it could be out of kindness. It could be a positive thing for you to hear. The word "no" can promote growth; it can help people rethink the goals they have set for themselves.

Being able to say "no" to people can also be considered an act of kindness. By saying "no" to someone who wants you to do something for them because they feel that they cannot succeed at the task themselves and would prefer if you could do it, you are showing them an act of kindness, and it will help them to succeed in whatever they have told themselves they cannot do. Saying that you cannot do it for them allows them to appreciate the possibility that they can do it for themselves. They may fail; however, they may succeed if given the opportunity.

Sometimes people need to hear the word "no" so they can grow the wings they need to soar in life. That means you believe in them enough to use the word "no" as an act of kindness to show them that you believe in them and you have faith that they can and will succeed. Only if they say "yes" to your "no," though—that is their challenge and the opportunity of kindness you have provided them with.

"Life challenges are not supposed to paralyze you,
they are supposed to help you discover who you are."
—Bernice Johnson Reagon

My life experiences are my greatest strength, no matter the opportunity or challenge. Even if you do not receive an opportunity for every challenge you face, it does not mean you will not have the opportunity in the future to use your life experiences. You may have a chance in some other aspect of your life, for someone else that has gone through almost the same situation as yours or experienced a challenge like yours. I say, "someone else may have gone through almost the same situation" because the other person will not have the same feelings, and the journey will be totally different for them. The way they look at and experience life is different from your own perspective. This is very important to realize for you, and for the person or people who walked a similar journey as yours. Everyone sees things through a different lens. Your children, grandchildren, neighbours, and friends do not ever understand how you look at things and see them so differently, even if the person was on the same journey as the one you walked.

That is why I feel that my life experiences would be helpful to people who want to know what kept me going. I didn't give up, and it was the strength for faith, courage, and hope that kept me going, and also because my family needed me. I could never give up on them, and I know they did not ever give up on me. They were my cheerleading team, and when the road became a jagged, rocky mess of steepness to climb, they helped me climb. They helped me stay strong, and without their gifts, without their love and faith, I could never have endured the heartache and pain that one endures watching and loving a family member walk their last journey of a lifetime. I believe I had a purpose, and I believe that life is sometimes unexplainable. I am grateful for my strength, courage, love, and kindness that I could show my family when they needed me the most. I was there, and I do not think I needed to be anywhere else in that moment in time. I am always happy when I can take the time to count my many blessings and say thank you to the people who gave me the strength to get up and wipe my tears. I am so blessed with all that I have in life, and continue to have. There is no better gift in this world than the love of family, and for that I am grateful. I have found peace, love, hope, and happiness in my minutes, moments, and new tomorrows that I thought were gone.

"Don't let your ears hear what your eyes didn't see,
and don't let your mouth say what your heart doesn't feel."
—Unknown

Close Your Eyes and Listen

Close your eyes and listen to your heartbeat. Listen to your heart, and concentrate on every beautiful beat. Do not listen to the noises in the room or the noise you hear outside. Have you ever stopped to listen to hear your heart beating? Some people go through a day, a week, a year, a lifetime, and they never stop to hear their own heartbeat. They have no idea what it should sound like for them. They have no idea if there is anything they should be listening for, because they have never stopped to hear the precious beats of their very own heart. Go somewhere quiet and sit down, then lie down, close your eyes, and listen to your heart. Take the time out of your busy day to be quiet and listen to the sounds that you take for granted. Listen to the beating of your heart, hear the calmness, and feel the calmness. You are now in touch with yourself—your peaceful, quiet mind. You can take a few minutes out of your busy day to get in touch with yourself to feel the peace and quiet of your life at this moment and in this time. The world has stopped for a few short minutes without you, and you can listen to your body and what it needs.

This is taking the time out of your busy day to show yourself a few minutes of kindness with the intention of re-energizing your mind, body, and soul so you can feel refreshed and continue to do what you do in the workplace and at home, and so you can offer someone a piece of kindness from your heart to theirs in case they need it. It is you taking care of you so you will feel and be in touch with your life experiences, as well as everyone else's life experiences that you are asked to help with. It is important for you to always be in touch with your inner self so you can reach out and be kind to anyone that may need kindness at any given moment in time.

"I ask not for a lighter burden, but for broader shoulders."
—Jewish Proverb

People say you can never judge a person unless you walk a mile in their shoes, and that is the most honest statement I have ever heard. I have learned the true value of my life and what is important to me as I reflect on moving forward into the future—or at least the near future. I do not plan for weeks or months ahead in my life, as I cannot look that far forward. I believe it is much easier to say I can plan for this moment, this hour, this day in time, and the future means the day ahead, or possibly the week.

Death has changed me, and there is nothing harder than death to bring your focus into what is important in life. No one can ever understand what kind of a journey I was on and how it affected my heart mind and soul. Most of us in this world fear death, and most of us are afraid of the unknown; however, for me it seems that life is the bigger challenge—learning to live without the people in my life who offered me so much unconditional love is sometimes harder to endure than thinking about or fearing death.

Death comes to us all, and you do not want to have a scroll of things that you did not get to finish or things that were left undone that you wished you had done. I think my family shared their dreams and wishes for me, and they all wanted me to be able to move forward.

I can say now that I am moving forward, and whatever my future holds I know I will be able to accomplish whatever lies ahead, as I have learned there is no problem in life greater than death. Everyone dies—it does not matter who you are, or how rich or how poor. The only thing that matters is that you have no regrets left on your plate when this day comes. My point is living in the moment, being in the moment, and staying true to your values and who you really are, because in the end that is your legacy. That is what you have left the world. Your passion for kindness, your love of people, the seeds you sow, the new beginnings that you have planted, and the new ideas in your children and grandchildren: these are the seeds for kindness, a better tomorrow, and a future filled with hope.

Wendy Comeau

"Coming together is a beginning; keeping together
is progress; working together is success."
—Henry Ford

Personal Life Stories

A Heart of Kindness

"Strength lies in differences, not in similarities."
—Stephen R Covey

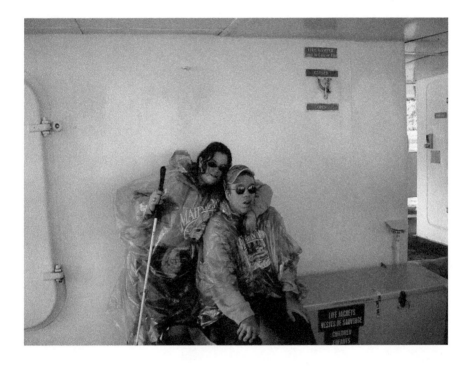

Jennifer & Christopher

Wendy Comeau

"There was never a night or a problem that could defeat
sunrise or hope."
—Bernard Williams

Sunrise from our balcony in Toronto, Ontario, Canada.

"Man never made any material as resilient as the human spirit."
—Bernard Williams

Smith's Rock on Fitzpatrick Mountain, Nova Scotia, Chalet 10, gave us the best memories we could ever experience.

"Smile, it is the key that fits the lock of everybody's heart."
-Anthony J. D'Angelo

A Wish and a Prayer

Christopher wanted to go home to Nova Scotia for his birthday. We knew this would be our last road trip as a family, and we were determined to make his wishes come true. We packed up the car with all the equipment that Christopher would need for a couple of weeks and headed out. Jennifer was the co-pilot, helping with the driving and her other multitasking skills that we all needed at different times throughout the trip.

I had no idea how this was going to work, maybe on a wish and a prayer, but we were going to find a place that would be able to accommodate Christopher's wheelchair and equipment. It ended up that the Gunn family's Stonehame Chalets (now Smith's Rock Chalets) on Fitzpatrick Mountain would be our destination, thanks to everyone there. It was a memory of a lifetime. We could relax and enjoy the campfires, the quietness of the days and evenings, and the nature was all around us. We found kindness at Fitzpatrick Mountain—the kindness of strangers and the understanding of what we were trying to do with the moments we had left to cherish. There is no better gift that anyone could have provided us with at that moment. The Gunn family seemed to understand, and I am not sure how they knew, but they left a card and a gift on the table for

"Don't cry because it's over, smile because it happened."
—Dr. Seuss

Christopher's twenty-fifth birthday. Sometimes your dreams do come true, and things fall into place when you least expect it. I am grateful for those last few weeks of memories, and I know Jennifer and Robert are, as well. Our memories are richer with this trip we could take with Christopher—the road trip we knew meant everything to everyone in his life. We were all able to be together one last time as a family to celebrate Halloween, Christopher's birthday, and Thanksgiving. It is hard to believe we poured so much into just a few short weeks, but we did, and it was worth every moment we shared as a family. That was our trip of a lifetime. Those few short weeks have been our best memories of everyone laughing and talking around a campfire.

I miss Nova Scotia, the ocean, and the memories of our family. Sometimes the memories we made of our life together seems like those days would never end. I am glad Christopher could have his last wish, and I am happy that it was in such a beautiful spot with nature and horses. Our memories with family will always keep me remembering and treasuring our minutes and moments in time. This was Christopher's last wish—the gift of his family that he cherished so much at such a young age. Thank you for all the wonderful memories you have left us with. Thank you for helping us to be brave and remember you are with us always.

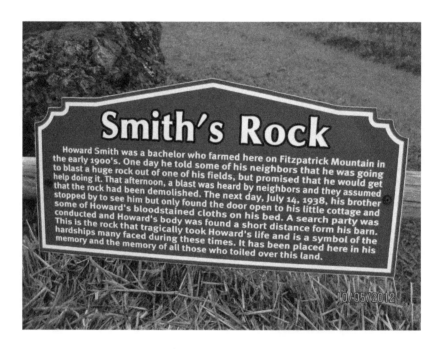

Smith's Rock on Fitzpatrick Mountain, Nova Scotia.

"A comfort zone is a beautiful place, but nothing ever grows there."
—Unknown

Back to School

One day, after thirty-six years, I decided I would go like back to school. I was interested in doing something in the helping field. It was an experience like no other I will ever have in my life. After what I had already experienced, I cannot explain why I was not surprised, except to say it opened my eyes to a whole new world of how people see things from their own perspective, and how their own needs were so much greater than anyone or anything else in the world. I had an insight into a kind of life I was unfamiliar with. I could not believe the vast amount of perspectives I had at my disposal. Many of the professors were fantastic: the knowledge, passion, and enthusiasm they had for teaching their classes was beyond anything that anyone could ever wish for—especially in the early morning classes.

When I walked into one professor's Mental Health and Addictions class, I thought, *how is she ever going to teach a subject that is so sensitive to so many*? The answer to that is that she taught it with passion—it mattered to her. People mattered. She had a heart for what she was saying. She told stories of what she had experienced in her life working in her field of study. She was funny and serious when she needed to be, and I don't know many people who would have a sense of ha! ha! after teaching and working as hard as she did at getting her point across. I am glad I sat in her class, as I think it gave me a deeper understanding into people and why life can be harder than it needs to be sometimes. I kept her PowerPoint presentations (she had a vast amount of them), and I kept the notes from her class. Whoever thought I could sit down and read and re-read something so many times to get the answers I was searching for in my own life?

She had experience—lived experiences—and after spending two semesters in her classes, I am grateful I had the opportunity to really listen to the messages she offered. She made everyone feel included; the conversations were open discussions in her class, and people's opinions mattered to her. She listened to everyone's opinion and did not ever seem offended by what anyone had to say. She offered up her opinion and addressed why she thought you could look at something in a different light.

A Heart of Kindness

"When people talk, listen completely. Most people never listen."
—Ernest Hemingway

You could tell she had passion for what she was teaching. You had the impression that she slept, ate, and believed in what she was saying—in her words and in what she was doing. She believed in people, and she had compassion for her students and the people around her. I loved listening to what she was going to say next; her in-depth explanations and her opinion all fit together and made sense.

"If you cannot be positive, then at least be quiet."
—Joel Osteen

Does Murphy Always Have to Come Along for the Ride?

Murphy's Law is: "If anything can go wrong, it will go wrong." It's an old expression I have heard forever. My question is, who the heck is Murphy, anyway, to always be poking his nose into our life? "That is what I want to know," I screamed and shouted at my husband. I do not mind the odd mishap in my life, but for every road you walk down, every turn you take, does Murphy really need to come along for the walk or ride? When I look back on the many journeys of my life, I think there are more Murphys than not. Why is that? Did I not ever plan for Plan A to work out? I always seemed to be going from Plan A to "let's just skip A and move down to Plan Z and we should have it right by then." I must say, I often thought life was a challenge.

You may be wondering what I am rambling on about—well, let me just share a few highlights of my life with you. I grew up with three brothers, and they were awesome—most of the time. However, we did seem to find trouble, or trouble found us. My youngest brother was practicing his pitching for baseball using large river rocks in the yard behind a little hill or mound when he accidently hit me in the eye with the rock. My eye was black and every colour of the rainbow for weeks; it was a horrible sight. On a positive note, my brother had to do all my chores for a week, including the dishes.

My mom asked my dad to go to the store and pick me out a pair of shoes that would match what I had on, because we had to attend a function at the army base. My dad was so excited when he came home with the shoes, but they were blue—bright blue; what the heck? I was ten years old! My mom shook her head, saying, "Wendy, do not hurt your dad's feelings. Wear the shoes." My gosh. I was wearing pink and green, and I had to look at my feet and see these bright blue shoes. Really, who is this Murphy, anyway? I looked like a Christmas tree. What were my parents thinking?

Years later, in September 2003, my dad died. However, that Christmas, I still received a special gift from my dad. He had always started his shopping early. It was really shocking to open the gift and find a Royal Daulton ornament; it was a father and daughter wedding dance, and the father was wearing blue shoes. The card inside said, *Wendy, thank you for wearing my blue shoes. Love, Dad.* My mom had found the gift under the bed all wrapped with my name on it and decided to wait until Christmas to give it to me. That was the last gift I received from my dad. It is not a sad story to me. It seems that my dad always had to have the last word, no matter what.

"It is our choices . . . that show what we truly are,
far more than our abilities."
—J. K. Rowling

On our last trip to New York with our son, we lost his wheel-chair. How can anyone lose a wheelchair? My husband, our nurse, and I were getting Christopher into the car, getting everything hooked up and making Christopher comfortable. It was rainy, windy, cold, and dark. I jumped out of the car to start putting the chair away and looked around. Where was the chair? "It's there outside the door," my husband said to me. "I am going to put it away now."

"No, you are not putting it away," I said. "The chair is gone. That chair cost us more than a good used car. What happened?" As I was having this conversation, Christopher was laughing at me. Our nurse quietly said we were in New York, and anything was possible. That is right—anything is possible. The wind had picked the chair up and blown it across the parking lot into a huge puddle, where it tipped it over. I must say, I often thought life was a challenge. But with every Murphy's Law there are always positive lessons to take away from Murphy, and believe me, there are wonderful lessons you will savour for a lifetime. Looking back over the years, I find some of these stories quite amusing; however, at the time you are experiencing Murphy it can be a little hard to find his humour.

"Don't walk behind me; I may not lead. Don't walk in front of
me; I may not follow. Just walk beside me and be my friend."
—Albert Camus

Our Moving Adventure

Everyone has moved at least once in their life, I am sure.
In my opinion, moving can be an adventure, or you can turn
it into the most stressful time of your life. Most people do not
have the money to hire a moving van when they are moving
across the country unless they have a government job, are
well established in their career, or are lucky enough to come
from a well-to-do family.

Me? I was not one of the lucky ones. I had to turn moving
into an adventure. Our first moving experience from Halifax
to Edmonton, Alberta, was the adventure I could have done
without. It was in January, it was cold, and I had to drive my
car across Canada with my daughter, who was four years old,
and two dogs, while my husband drove a U-Haul. This was
the first time for me driving across Canada by myself without
a co-pilot to read the map. I had my doubts that this trip would
go as smoothly as my husband thought it would. My first clue
was when he was paying for the U-Haul; he laid an envelope
full of money down on the counter and walked away. I did not
say a word, and just picked it up.

We left that sunny morning for Edmonton. What a trip. I was
terrified of driving through Montreal at any time. Lunch-hour

traffic was the worst. I managed to stay in the right lane and hit the La Fontaine Tunnel, and I certainly was utterly shocked when I got it right the first time out. I asked Jennifer if she could see her daddy, and she said, "Yes, I see him. He is one car behind us." I said okay, and told her to keep an eye on the U-Haul. What was I thinking? She was four years old, so how was she to know one U-Haul from all the other ones on the road? I was halfway to Ottawa before I realized it was the wrong U-Haul—it was not her dad.

I was starting to panic. What should I do now, short of having a meltdown? Remember, this was before cell phones. I turned the car around and did a trip back through Montreal feeling quite nervous. I had to still be positive and pretend I knew what I was doing. I did not see my husband; however, he did see me. He was sitting in a police car on the side of the road, because the U-Haul had run out of gas. The officer had ordered up gas to be delivered by a tow truck, and the tow truck driver had to take my husband to a bank, as I had picked up the envelope full of cash; he hadn't noticed he'd left it on the counter, so he had no cash. I drove up and down that highway three times and could not spot him. I made an executive decision to keep driving through to Ottawa, and when I did, I spotted him driving in front of me.

"The community which has neither poverty nor riches
will always have the noblest principles."
—Plato

We stopped for a half-hour break to regroup. The truck
stopped dead again in Winnipeg in the middle of the ring
road, and it was -50° outside. What we did not realize was
that the gas gauge did not work on that U-Haul. I was ready to
stop, myself. My patience was wearing very thin. I asked my
husband if there was really anything in this truck we needed,
because I was ready to dump the truck. He looked at me and
said, "Are you okay? Because this is everything we own, and
Jennifer needs her stuff—namely, her bed."

I looked at him and said, "Do you know what I need? I need
a truck that works. One that has gas." I could not believe
anyone would rent us a truck with a gas gauge that did not
work. I was exhausted, and the weather was so cold and
windy the dogs would not even get out of the car. I could see
my husband was stressed, and I said, "Okay, you are right.
We are almost to Edmonton, so let's get this trip behind us."

I was being positive and trying to find some humour in all of
this when Jennifer said, "Daddy, can I have ice cream and an
adventure when we get to Edmonton?"

He looked at her and said, "You can you can have anything
you want, kiddo."

"Change is hard at first, messy in the middle, and gorgeous at the end."
—Robin Sharma

Change

It is hard to make changes when we are afraid of the unknown. Life changes all the time; nothing stays the same forever. After much reflection about this, I remembered my dad saying to me when I complained, "Wendy, you can always change anything in your life that makes you unhappy; you get to write your own story." Wow, Dad, thanks. I understood exactly what he meant, because I really needed to change my life to heal. It is an understatement to say how sad and broken inside I felt as each day passed. I kept thinking how unfair life was—but then, life is not fair. It is unrealistic to think it should be.

I needed to leave my comfort zone. My first step was talking with my husband, and we decided I needed to do something with my life. I had been a stay-at-home-mom for twenty-five years, so I thought I just needed to get out of the house and do something. That was my first step toward change. I had not been in a school in thirty-six years (unless you count the parent–teacher meetings and the pizza and popcorn sales).

My next big change was to sell the home we had lived in for seventeen years. It was a hard decision to make; however, I needed to make this change. We decided we would move out of Barrie, where we had lived for twenty-nine years. My husband had been driving up and down the highway that whole time to Toronto. We sold the house, and that was not without difficulty. We did not realize how hard it would be to paint our son's bedroom and pack up a house full of memories. We were standing in the bedroom saying, "You put the paint on the wall first," and we went back and forth for about five minutes until I picked up the gallon of paint and threw it on the wall. Then we both had to make the change at the same time.

What I am trying to say here is life is hard—sometimes devastating, but what I have learned is that I had a choice. I could change my life and find a little piece of happiness, or I could have stayed in the messy middle forever. Change is good. If you do not like something in your life, no matter how big or small it is, change it.

"Only I can change my life. No one can do it for me."
—Carol Burnett

Bring balance, happiness, and joy back into your life. You oversee your life story; you are the one that gets to write it. In the end, change is gorgeous!

"After all this is over, all that will have really
mattered is how we treated each other."
—Unknown

The Paper Towel Communication

Communication is very important in everything we do in our lives, no matter where you are or what you choose to do. When you lack good communication skills, it can cause a domino effect when handling some situations, and things that seem simple can quickly deteriorate. You may ask yourself, "What is communication?" Communication is simply the transferring of information from one place to another using voice, writing, websites, or e-mails, just to name a few. I always thought I was a good communicator until one Christmas Eve when I ask my husband Robert to hand me a wet piece of paper towel.

This could have made some people tear out their hair. I could have crawled out from under where I was and done it myself—that would have been the simplest solution at the time. I was thinking, *How can my husband not understand me? What the heck is wrong with what I am saying*? After being with someone for so many years, you would think your partner would understand you—no, not so much, apparently. I thought my communication skills were not lacking when I said to him, "Robert, could you lift the glass out of the dining room table so I can clean up the last of the glitter spilled earlier?" No problem with that communication. Then I said, "Could you please bring me a piece of wet paper towel?" Simple enough? No: it was totally misunderstood. The first time, my husband brought me a piece of paper towel that was wet in the top corner. I looked at him and said, "Are we short of water? Look at what I must clean." I was trying to pick up the glitter I had spilled making a last-minute ornament for a guest who had decided to come after all, and I did not want to get glitter on the floor and then stop and clean the floor. I was running out of time before our friends and family came over. I looked at my husband and said, "I would like a piece of wet paper towel. Wet it, please, then wring it out and bring it to me. Thank you."

"The biggest single problem in communication
is the illusion that it has taken place."
—George Bernard Shaw

I was looking down at the table using the piece of partially wet paper towel and concentrating on the glitter when out of the corner of my eye, I saw Robert come back into the room. I looked up and my husband was holding the paper towel. My exact words were, "Really? Really? Are you kidding me?" He was not understanding me—or he had, without my knowledge, had some kind of bang to his head. Something had happened, because this is what he had in his hand: a roll of paper towel. Yes, that is right, a brand-new roll of paper towel, sopping wet and partially wrung out. I was half-laughing and saying, "Are you serious?"

He looked at me and said, "You really must learn to explain more clearly what you are asking for."

I said, "What part of the conversation did you get lost in? I asked for a piece of wet paper towel wrung out. Where in the conversation did you hear a roll of paper towel wrung out? And if you do not want to waste my time, you should think before you speak, because we have fifteen people coming in less than two hours."

He looked at me and said, "Wendy, you need to learn to explain in more detail what you are asking."

I said, "Tonight, my dear friend, you are going to be the topic of conversation. I am going to give everyone a small roll of paper towel and a piece of paper towel at their place setting. I am going to ask them to wet me a piece of paper towel and wring it out and bring it back to the table. You will not explain why we are doing this until after it is over, and then you can see how many people used a piece of paper towel, and how many used a roll of paper towel. Please do not mention what happened until after everyone has sat down again. We will see how many took the roll of paper towel or the piece of paper towel."

Afterwards, everyone sat back at the table, and we counted who had used the piece of paper towel, and who had used the roll of paper towel. The results were not surprising to me. The count was fifteen pieces of wet paper towel and zero rolls used. This proved that my communication skills were not lacking in this situation. Communication is important, and we should try to test ourselves occasionally to make sure we have communicated and listened to what people are saying. I know it could have made a difference for me. My husband told his story, and everyone had a good laugh.

"Sometimes you will never know the value
of the moment until it becomes a memory."
—Dr. Seuss

Home for the Holidays!

No matter where we were living, we always went home for the holidays. One year, my husband and I drove in from Edmonton with Jennifer, who was two years old at the time. Our destination was Halifax, Nova Scotia. We were the first to arrive. My parents always knew we would be coming home, but they never knew what day. My husband and I loved road trips—they were about unwinding and just relaxing and enjoying our surroundings and the beauty of each province as we drove through them in the winter. The trips were amazing.

My dad and I decided to put up the tree before my mom came home from work and before my brothers arrived home. We thought this would be easy, but was I wrong. My dad always surprised me with some of his ideas sometimes. *I would be like, really, Dad, are you kidding me? Mom is going to lose it.* This is how my dad solved problems: with hammers, nails, or a saw. I used to think, *Okay, do not ever try this at my house, Dad.* The carpet in the house was so thick that the tree would not stand up, and my dad decided he wanted to put the tree in this one corner of the living room. All I could do was shake my head and tell my husband not to ever try this at home.

"You're on your own. And you know what you know.
And you are the one who'll decide where to go."
—Dr. Seuss

My dad went and got the hammer and three spikes, and he spiked the tree to the floor and the wall. I had taken my eyes off Jennifer for a few minutes, as I was so focused on my dad that I had totally forgotten about my child. Then I was startled at the sound of, "Oh God!" Yes, my mom's voice saying, "Has everyone lost total grip with reality?"

I said, "Mom, I tried to . . ." and she pointed to what Jennifer was doing. I turned, and Jennifer was standing on the dining room table having the time of her life. She had found something totally intriguing to entertain her. She did not need one toy . . . oh no. I said, "This is your granddaughter, Dad. She is two, and look, she is already like you." Oh my gosh; she had taken the crystal chandler apart piece by piece. I went to the table and said to Jennifer, "What are you doing?"

The answer I received was clearly not what I expected, however. She said, "I wanted to see the colours and hold them." The sun was shining on the chandler, and she wanted to see all the colours. I thought, Okay, *let's get this light back together* after stopping to hug my mom and make eye contact with my husband so he would know to please fix the light. My mom was saying the tree was nice and straight and asked my dad if he picked the board up she ordered, knowing full well he had not, because it was still in the trunk of the car.

My mom clearly knew the tree was spiked to the wall with a clear piece of twine, and you could see the spike marks in the carpet. Yes, my dad nailed the tree stand to the floor. My husband looked at me and said, "Wendy, do we need to go for a drive?"

I said, "No. Watch how my mom solves problems."

All my mom said was, "You realize the room will need to be painted and new carpet will need to go down after Christmas." The doorbell rang at the right moment, and as my youngest brother appeared, all I could think was, *really, dad?* and my brother said, "Wendy, is this why you came home? To be the first one to deal with the tree?" "Look at Jennifer."

"Here's to strong women, may we know them, may we raise them, may we be them."—Unknown

My Daughter's Wedding Day

My daughter got married on Saturday, September 17, 2016. What a whirlwind day that turned out to be. The first dilemma, we thought, was the weather; but no, it was not. Jennifer put everything into its right perspective. It turned out to be an awesome day. Imagine the look on my face when she told the photographer and videographer she wanted pictures she could remember and appreciate for a lifetime. It was pouring down raining—what kind of pictures are you talking about? I was thinking, *Oh no, we know how creative Jennifer can be, and when she uses her imagination, nothing is impossible.* Has anyone ever heard of trashing the dress before the reception? No, I did not think so. The photographer and videographer said, "Would you like to take your shoes off and stand in a puddle?"

Jennifer said, "Where is my mom? She will have a stroke when she sees this." I totally missed that picture. The next time I looked up, she was running and jumping in this big huge puddle with the camera rolling and the wedding party standing by cheering her on. I was too far away to completely see what she was doing. Then she came back to where Robert and I were standing, and someone had passed her a towel to wipe the mud off her feet so she could put her shoes on.

The next picture was of her standing on this picnic table, and I thought, *how beautiful is this day?* Jennifer stood and looked up almost defiantly, as if to say, *Rain, pour, I am going to have the memories from this day.*

"You have to accept whatever comes, and the only important thing is that you meet it with courage, and with the best that you have to give."
—Eleanor Roosevelt

Nothing that happened that day was staged; everything was natural and just seemed to happen the way it was supposed to. Everyone was relaxed; there were pictures and tears, and the day all came together. It felt like the rain belonged there with us. It felt like the heavens had opened and said, *finally it's your day, be happy, be creative with your life. It is yours to have and yours to mould and create as you want it to be.* Jennifer looked beautiful; she looked almost like a china doll from across the room. The day was finally here, and Jennifer could breathe, laugh, smile, and have the dance of her life. We made the memories that Jennifer so wanted that day. We toasted to new beginnings.

We all shared a quiet moment for the family members who were not there in body, but we knew they were with us, and we could feel the joy, for everything happens for a reason, and the rain that fell that day was our family blessings for Jennifer's new beginning. I said earlier in the day that when it rains on the bride's wedding day, you will be blessed and that all the negativity will wash away. I can say that it was the most beautiful day ever.

"Learn from yesterday, live for today, hope for tomorrow. The important thing is not to stop questioning."
—Albert Einstein

Who Inspires You and Why?

Ask yourself this question: Who inspires you and why? Does someone come to mind right off the top of your head? Is that person unique? Can you pick them out of a crowded room? I am asking this question for several reasons: one is that there are a lot of different people who have inspired me throughout my life. They have believed in me and supported me at different times, and this includes my parents. I want to share this story with you about a person who inspired me; her message to me was about hope. I have had the opportunity to meet a lot of people over the years that inspired me. What makes people unique and stand up and want to make a difference for themselves and others?

Well, I found the answer to my question when I had an opportunity to meet and have dinner with a dear friend's mom. Her name is Elsa Thon, and she wrote the book *If Only It Were Fiction*. I have read the book several times over the years, and I always found something different or took another lesson from the book every time I read it. Elsa was born on January 10, 1923, in Poland. It was on her sixteenth birthday that the Germans invaded Poland in the Second World War. She spent the better part of the war in a concentration camp and lost her entire family.

At dinner, we spoke about her book, and her courage. I asked Elsa, "What made you able to keep going?"

These are her words to me: "Wendy, *hope* kept me going, because every day when the sun came up it was a new day, and a new day meant hope. Hope kept me going, and hope, Wendy, will keep you going. Never give up hope." Elsa said that when there is life, there is hope, and if we all have hope, anything in life is possible. We talked about her husband, her children, grandchildren, and great-grandchildren. She told me she wrote the book so the history would not die with her. The history needs to be told and retold so the atrocities will never happen again. For someone to lose so much at such a young age and to live to tell about it is a gift. Our dinner went on for three hours. There were three other people at dinner with us, but for some reason, not trying to be rude, she said, "I just want to talk with Wendy." *Hope* is what keeps people going—it feeds them when they are hungry, cold, and in pain, emotionally as well as physically.

"You cannot do a kindness too soon, for you never
know how soon it will be too late."
—Ralph Waldo Emerson

Elsa is an inspiration for everyone who knows her or has had the opportunity to read her book. She is my hope; in my opinion, she has given a lot to the world. She has said to me, "Wendy, the world is a different place now, and things have changed." Her father told her that with hope, tomorrow can always be a better day. If you give up, you will never know if today would have been that better day, and she never gave up hope. "Wendy, never ever give up hope." That was her message to me.

The next time you have a chance to speak with someone, ask yourself what is unique or inspirational about the people you meet. Who do you inspire and leave with a lasting impression? I would like to leave you with this thought: remember, with hope, tomorrow is always a new day, and anything is possible.

"You are braver than you believe. Stronger than you seem. Smarter than you think, and loved more than you know."
—Unknown

Exploring Independence

This is a small glimpse of how we grew with our daughter as she grew through different stages of her life. I said to my husband, "Remember when we thought our daughter would never stop exploring and finding trouble?" It is an understatement, to say the least, that someone would say our children need to be explorers to learn to become independent. This is my view of our child exploring and becoming independent.

The worst, I thought, was what everyone referred to as the terrible twos. *Can I trade my child in?* I thought. My child looked adorable, cute—what a beautiful child she was. However, please remember, your child does not come with directions; you cannot take them back to the store for a refund. No, you will not get a refund.

We were in the Kmart with Jennifer, who had a meltdown in the middle of the aisle. I was thinking, *What now*? I just wanted to get in and out of the store as quickly as possible.

This was 100% my father's fault—what the heck was he thinking, telling his two-year-old granddaughter you can buy a baby at the Kmart for a quarter? My dad gave Jennifer a dollar to buy four babies. That was just the start of many episodes to come.

"Trust yourself. Create the kind of self that you will be happy to live with all your life. Make the most of yourself by fanning the tiny, inner sparks of possibility into flames of achievement."

—Golda Meir

Jennifer, at four years old, thought she would like to start her day off by being creative and make a cake first thing in the morning to help me out. I was busy making beds and throwing the first load of laundry in to get ahead of my day. It is only 7:00 a.m. Jennifer was busy making a cake on the new couch that was not quite a week old. All I could think when I discovered what she was doing was *Thank God, this couch is on wheels*. At that point, I had two options: wheel it out to the kitchen and try to clean it, or out the front door to the street. I chose the street. Why, you might ask? The ingredients for the cake: a dozen eggs, a five-pound bag of oatmeal, two quarts of milk, and a bottle of honey—oh yes, we had to have honey on everything back then. I remember thinking, *Can I go back to bed and start this day again?* Really, what can you do? You cannot blame the child, because you were down the hall making beds and throwing a load in the laundry. What was I thinking? I seemed to ask the question a lot of myself. This was obviously her creative side, so do not challenge that, I told myself. You do not want to take away her passion or creativity. At six, Jennifer wanted to bring pussy willows into the house where we were living in Edmonton, Alberta, at the time. I said, "No, you cannot bring the pussy willows into the house."

Jennifer said to me, "Why, Mommy? Why are you being so unreasonable?"

I was not in the mood for debating with her after a long day. All I said was, "Because pussy willows will turn into pussycats if you bring them into the house." Again, what was I thinking?

On Saturday morning, we went to the pool for swimming lessons. The Grade Two science teacher was there, and he came over to me and said, "Mrs. Comeau, nice to see you here. I was hoping you could tell me how pussy willows turn into pussycats when you bring them into the house. I had a debate with Jennifer in class, and she insisted that they do. I told her, 'Whatever your mommy tells you, Jennifer, is right. Listen to your mom.'"

Jennifer is going to be exploring the world of marriage now. We have allowed her to explore, to learn, to become independent, to hope, to believe, to dream, and oh yes, most of all, we have allowed her to be creative. I can say we have done our job well. Jennifer and Darrell—congratulations! Explore and grow together, always believe in each other, be happy, and Jennifer: never stop being awesome. Love, Mommy & Dad.

"If you are always racing to the next moment,
what happens to the moment you are in?"
—Unknown

Robert and I were driving along the highway, coming back from a fun-filled day at the water slides in Sylvan Lake, Alberta, with Jennifer when she was six years old. We were driving back to Edmonton on what was then called the Calgary Trail late at night. Robert decided that he was tired and I was going to take over and drive for a while. We were both sunburnt— very burnt, as those were the days you would fry your skin with baby oil and get the best tan possible. As Robert was pulling off to the side of the road for us to trade places, he hit a board—a 2x4, to be exact. Apparently, a truck driver lost part of his load and the board went right through the radiator of the car. Well, that was a perfect end to our great day. It was pitch black outside, and we were in the middle of nowhere, but we could see a light in the distance. How far in the distance? Two miles, to be exact. This was before the time of cell phones or any kind of technology. The only technology back then when something happened was the use of your feet— you got the privilege of walking to get help. My husband said, "See the light? I will walk and get help. You and Jennifer lock the doors and I will be back soon."

"NOOOO," I said. "No way. I am not staying here in this car while you walk. It could be farther than you think. The lights could very well be miles and miles away, and that is not an option for us . . . you are not leaving us behind."

Well, just imagine everything from Jennifer's point of view—she was six years old, and she said, "Daddy, you can push the car and Mommy can steer it." Believe it or not, that is what we did. It took forever, as it was exactly two miles down the road. That trip was the most expensive trip to a water park ever. We had to have the car towed back to Edmonton and repaired, so it was a total of $1000.00.

"The greatest glory in living lies not in never falling,
but rising every time we fall."
—Nelson Mandela

Toastmasters

I joined Toastmasters on November 1, 2015, after a pro-fessor suggested it to me. I was doing a presentation in her class on an article from the paper, and my assignment was to speak about the article and explain the importance of it. I was so nervous I felt sick, and the professor allowed me to sit on the desk and speak to the class. I felt the fear of speaking that day and many days after that until I took her suggestion and joined the Toastmasters Club.

I did not have a clue what Toastmasters was until I went in and talked to the people and experienced it for myself. I thought it was the best-kept secret ever. It was one of the best suggestions I have received in a very long time. I enjoy all the feedback and encouragement that everyone provides, with the extension of friendship included. Everyone is there to encourage you to do your best, and they are always willing to listen to your point of view and suggest where you can improve and do better. Whether it is for your next speech at Toastmasters or a speech you are preparing for outside the club, they are there to help you build your confidence and speak with ease. I could make a speech at my daughter's wedding, and I know that before going to Toastmasters, that would never have happened. It makes you feel comfortable and confident to be able to get up and speak in front of a room full of people. They provide you with the support you need to help you to reach your goals with encouragement. Where else can you have laughs and learn the craft of speaking and education, all in a friendly environment?

I am grateful for the professor that suggested I could try Toastmasters, and I am grateful for my fellow Toastmasters friends I have made in the last couple of years. Toastmasters is about treating yourself with kindness to achieve the self-confidence you need to do the things that you never dreamed you could do because fear stood in the way. It has been a lot of fun at Toastmasters. Thank you to everyone at the club for helping me to grow and feel comfortable with speaking.

"My goal is to help people put value back into their life. To inspire everyone to dream, to explore through caring, believing and never judging themselves or others; life is about treating yourself with kindness."
—Wendy Bernadette Comeau

Being Prepared (Toastmasters Speech)

"In my opinion, you can be prepared for some things in life, but you cannot prepare for life. Life happens whether we are prepared or not. I can share with you how you can prepare for things that you can control in your life, and how you can overcome your fear and be prepared always when you are called upon to be a leader for anything in life. Ask yourself, why did you join Toastmasters? I joined to be able to speak with confidence; however, I also want to be able to connect with the people I am speaking with. I want them to clearly understand and connect to my message.

Everyone in this room has experienced fear over something, and it has stopped you from being able to move forward. Being prepared is an important part of overcoming your fear. Being unprepared sets yourself up for failure and leaves you feeling that you are a failure. However, if you use your words correctly, you are not a failure. You failed because you did not bother to read your book or do your homework. You are doing yourself a disservice. You are not setting yourself up for success, and you are not going to get the whole experience of Toastmasters. It is about planning and organizing for your speech or any job you are doing—if you are unprepared, you are setting yourself up for failure. What if you could over-come your fear? What if you could be prepared for what you fear the most? What if you could give your best speech at Toastmasters, or on a Table Topic subject? You can do it—yes, you can.

If you can imagine yourself at the bottom of a big hill and look up the hill, you are going to think, *I cannot get to the top of that hill. The hill is too long and steep. I will never make it. I am not prepared to climb a hill that big or that steep.* Your fear is, *I will not make it.* However, if you can imagine your-self at the top of the hill and you are looking down the hill, you are feeling empowered, you are feeling confident, you are feeling, *Wow, I can do anything. I am prepared. I can do this.* If you imagine yourself doing something that you want to accomplish, you will and can accomplish it. Your goal is to give a speech with confidence, and your fear is overpowering you. You are sending yourself a negative message to your subconscious that cannot change your negative

"It's not that I'm so smart, it's just that I stay with problems longer."
—Albert Einstein

thoughts. Your goal must be to feed yourself positive, kind words. You must change your words so that your thoughts can line up with your intentions, and your words then become positive self-talk.

Imagine you are going to give a speech tonight—you are going to imagine connecting with everyone in the room. You are going to make everyone feel like you are speaking to them and telling them *Yes, you can be the leader.* You will give an awesome speech by using your imagination and positive self-talk over and over until you feel it is not in your mind anymore—it has become a reality. You now believe you can give that speech without feeling the fear you felt a week ago, a day ago, or a minute ago. Believe you can, and because you believe you can, it will happen. Take the word "fear" out of your life and replace it with believe. I believe I can, so I did.

Being prepared is important to me.

Thank you, fellow Toastmasters.

Wendy Comeau

"Nothing is impossible, the word itself says I'm possible!"
—Audrey Hepburn

The Hair Salon

Did you know that when you go to a hair salon, you can feel so much better than when you walked in the door? I did not ever have that experience until I found this hair salon in my neighbourhood close to where I lived. The thing is, at this salon, it does not appear that anyone working there is working. What does this mean, you may ask? The ladies are happy. They have passion for what they do. They never appear to be unhappy with their jobs. They are always kind, and they listen to every person's idea of what they would like for a hairstyle. Sometimes they suggest some possibilities you may not have thought of for yourself. However, I have found that after going there for some time, things do not change at that salon—or should I say, the people who work there don't change. They are always kind, and they are always happy, friendly people. They believe it is important to feel good about yourself. If you are having a bad moment in your day, or had many bad moments in your day, and you have not gone to a hair salon lately, treat yourself to getting a makeover or a new hairstyle. You will not believe how much better you feel with a new look. Going out and doing some small things for yourself when you are feeling tired and need some tender, loving self-care or would like a change for yourself is the best thing to lift your spirits.

I took that step one day into this hair salon, and I am happy I did. It was the best day I'd had in a long time. I went in and talked to the lady, and she quickly thought about what I could do with my hair. I needed a change. I needed a new look. Every time you go into the salon and come out it feels like you have spent the day talking with old friends, and it is like a little family within the walls of a salon: a group of people caring about anyone walking through the doors.

On I think it was the second visit, I wanted to get my hair done and my eyebrows waxed. I was now at the age that I would get this waxing done every week. I asked the lady doing the waxing of my eyebrows and hair a question that caught her off-guard. I simply said, "Did you pull out the white hair in my eyebrow?" She had this expression on her face like she did not know what to say. She could not hide her look of, *oh no, what have I done*?

"For beautiful eyes, look for the good in others; for beautiful
lips, speak only words of kindness; and for poise,
walk with the knowledge that you are never alone."
—Audrey Hepburn

Worried that she may have done the wrong thing and I
might like the one white hair that was there in my eyebrow,
she looked confused and said, "Yes," not knowing if I would
be a returning customer. I looked at her face and we both had
a good laugh. I was happy with the "yes," because I wanted to
make sure it was gone before I left the salon. The salon stylist
thought I might be saving it.

Did you ever realize how dedicated and supportive they are to
people that come through their doors? It does not matter if you
are a first-time customer or have spent a lifetime going to the
same salon—they treat you with genuine kindness. They want
you to have the best experience, and to feel good in their salon.

It did not matter what was going on in their salon—someone
was always laughing and had a story to tell to brighten up your
day. Our hairdressers listen when you have something exciting
going on in life, and they create your hair for an event and make
you feel like you are the only one that is important now to them.
They make you feel good about what is happening in your life,
such as your special days, and they listen to your life happen-
ings with kindness and understanding. I think that at the salon
they believe that if you feel good about yourself, then you will
feel good about your life. Self-care and a new hairstyle can do
wonders for a new positive you and how you feel.

"We all make mistakes, have struggles, and even regret things in our past. But you are not your mistakes, you are not your struggles, and you are here now with the power to shape your day and your future."
—Steve Maraboli

Fresh Vegetables

One day I decided that, like every Saturday, we would go to the vegetable market in Bradford to buy our fresh fruits and vegetables. It was an outing, and it would be fun for the kids. I wanted fresh vegetables; like everyone else, I wanted to feed my children the best they could eat to grow and be healthy. Robert was not too sure about this after that day. He thought maybe we could have saved a bundle of money if I had gone to Sobeys and bought the vegetables like everyone else. I tried to explain how much nicer and fresher everything tasted from a garden this time of year, not to mention the nutrients we would be all benefitting from.

We did not seem to come out ahead that week. My Dodge Caravan was burning oil, and when he pulled out of the parking lot to leave the market, a police officer was parked across the street. He noticed and gave my husband a ticket for excessive smoke. The ticket cost us 150 dollars. Robert thanked the police officer and said to me, "I hope we all appreciate these fruits and vegetables, because that was one expensive trip to the vegetable market." I could not believe it.

Every time I made dinner I thought, *I hope the kids eat their vegetables.* It became more about not wasting the food since we received the ticket, which I don't think is ever in anyone's grocery budget.

I thought, *Okay, it is Saturday, and we will have to get my van in and get it fixed—there is no way we can put this off. I need something to drive, so we will price it and get it fixed.* We drove over to the garage and got an estimate on how much the van would cost to fix and headed home. We were at the set of lights when the most horrifying thing happened: the light turned green, and I said to my husband, "The light is green." I looked down and he was holding the steering wheel in his hand; it had detached from the steering column. The wires were all attached and the car was still running. It was, again, the worst weekend. However, we managed to look at each other and laugh.

"There is a crack in everything, that's how the light gets in."
—Leonard Cohen

My reaction was *You're kidding me—we just finished paying for the van, its warranty is up, and it is falling apart.* Robert managed to drive the vehicle and get it fixed. It was not in the budget to fix the smoking problem before the steering wheel; however, we needed the steering wheel first. We spent most of our life together making decisions and trying to spend money in places that needed the most priorities. Then we could deal with all the other little problems of life as they came. Sometimes things would happen and Robert would say, "Guess what? Things always work out. Let's not worry about this. It will work out. I don't know how, but it will." I appreciated the fact that Robert was not going to let things that happened in our day ruin our moments.

Life happens whether we are ready for it or not. It is about surviving and moving on to the next little moment and maybe, just maybe, the next moment in time will be a little bit kinder. Things are always going to happen while you are living life; it is how you think of the experience that will get you through it. If something happens in one moment to upset you, let go of it, do not hold on to the negative part of the experience. Find something positive and move forward. Do not stay in the past. You will feel much better about your experience.

Wendy Comeau

"When you love what you have, you have everything you need."
—Unknown

Why, Mommy, Why!

A lot of years ago, before her first day of kindergarten, Jennifer said to me, "Mommy, if you miss me while I am at school, you can walk across the street and watch me through the window." Looking back over the years at my life, it is amazing to me how much perspective our children had. I thought, *Wow, my four-year-old daughter thought I may be lonely.* When we have time in our life to reflect on what our children say to us, it is mind-boggling to me how smart and wise they are.

Jennifer was our child of determination; if she had an idea, it was not a question of will it work—it was *it will* work. Who was I to explain that it might or might not work? Who was I to deter her from her way of thought or her imagination? I was not ever going to tell my children they could not do something unless it affected someone else's wellbeing or their own safety.

Our children were always on the go. Jennifer started gymnastics at three and then discovered her passion for dance; she was an amazing dancer, and by the time she was finishing high school she knew what she wanted: to dance. If she could dream it, she did it. Jennifer never liked the word "no" when she was a child, and she certainly does not like it as an adult living her life

174

today. Her favourite word from the time she could speak was "why?" And today her favourite word as an adult is "why not?" Jennifer learned at an early age that life can be hard, and that life is full of disappointments, but that if you fall, it is important to get back up and do it until you get it right. Now, looking back, I think her world of dance and gymnastics taught her that discipline. She fell, she got up, and she danced until she was happy with her performance.

Jennifer also learned early in life that even though you want something and you practice, practice, practice, sometimes other people's challenges get in your way. Her dream of continuing her studies of dance and opening her own dance studio ended very quickly, because someone did not take a few minutes of thought to wonder what might happen if they drove their car while drinking. I think Jennifer has come to realize that you can do your best, be your best, and it will not always end up the way you plan or want life to turn out. You cannot plan life—life happens. You can plan your moments in life, but you cannot plan so far in advance that you cannot see past the tomorrows.

Wendy Comeau

"Wherever there is a human being, there is an opportunity
for kindness."
—Lucius Annaeus Seneca

"Saying nothing . . . sometimes says the most."
—Emily Dickinson

Give Lavishly, Live Abundantly

The more you give,
The more you get.
The more you laugh,
The less you fret.
The more you do unselfishly,
The more you live abundantly.
The more of everything you share,
The more you'll always have to spare.
The more you love,
The more you'll find
That life is good
And friends are kind,
For only what we give away,
Enriches us from day to day.

—Helen Steiner Rice

Footprints

One night a man had a dream. He dreamed he was walking along the beach with the LORD. Across the sky flashed scenes from his life. For each scene, he noticed two sets of footprints in the sand; one belonged to him, and the other to the LORD.

When the last scene of his life flashed before him, he looked back at the footprints in the sand. He noticed that many times along the path of his life there was only one set of footprints. He also noticed that it happened at the very lowest and saddest times in his life.

This really bothered him and he questioned the LORD about it. "Lord, you said that once I decided to follow you, you'd walk with me all the way. But I have noticed that during the most troublesome times in my life, there is only one set of footprints. I don't understand why when I needed you most you would leave me."

The Lord replied, "My precious, precious child, I love you and would never leave you. During your times of trial and suffering, when you see only one set of footprints, it was then that I carried you."

—Margaret Fishback Powers

The prayer "Footprints" hung on my bedroom wall when I was growing up. When I left home, I took it off the wall and carried it with me on the many journeys of my life. Sometimes I felt like the man in the prayer, but at a closer glance, I can say that sometimes that is all that sustains us in life: the faith and the trust that the Lord will carry us on our worst days when we think we cannot endure the trials and tribulations. Thank you, Mom, for teaching me that there is always a higher power, and whatever trials and tribulations I am going through, they too will pass.

"What's coming will come, and we'll just
have to meet it when it does."
—J. K. Rowling

Christopher & Robert

"Gratitude turns what we have into enough, and more. It turns denial into acceptance, chaos into order, confusion into clarity . . . it makes sense of our past, brings peace for today, and creates a vision for tomorrow."
—Melody Beattie

Gratitude

I am grateful for my parents teaching me never to give up on myself or anyone else.

I am grateful to have been able to walk a journey of a lifetime with my son when he was dying, with my husband, daughter, and family beside me.

I am grateful for my parents and everything they taught me about being a family.

I am grateful for my son being the brave one and showing me that love will always last a lifetime in my heart, even when he is not present in body.

I am grateful to be the one to be there for every family member that died.

I am grateful to have shared in the precious gift of family with my family.

I am grateful for my faith and hope for another day.

I am grateful for my mom telling me that those little things in life were little things and they will take care of themselves.

I am grateful for my daughter, Jennifer, who realizes no matter what happens in your life, life is good.

I am grateful for my friends that walked the journey beside me, or behind me; they were there to laugh, smile, and cry with me and listen—just listen.

I am grateful for every person I met that chose to walk with me on all the different journeys of my life.

I am grateful for the kindness, love, and support of my best friend and husband, Robert D'Orsay, who walked the many journeys of a lifetime with me, who never had to say anything to me at all, who said it with his eyes, and for the many years of highs and lows. I am grateful to have had him by my side. It seems that when the road got harder to walk and the journey got longer, he was my rock. Thank you for being my friend, my kindred spirit, and walking the journey of a lifetime with me. I will always cherish those hard moments and memories that we did not realize we were making.

However, even though I had all the support of my husband, family, friends, and strangers, I am most grateful for my faith. To have the strength and courage to pray for the hope I would need in my life for a tomorrow. That a new day would help me find my faith in a higher power God and move forward from an experience I will always treasure.

Even though I am grateful for my journey and my gifts of walking this journey of a lifetime with my son, my dad, my mother, and brothers, I must say it was a journey no one ever wishes to walk, but I am glad I did. I am thankful I was the one that was given that gift from God, my higher power, to walk this journey with my family.

These are the things I am most grateful for. These were my gifts and blessings that were bountiful in my life. These were the gifts and blessings I thought I had lost with each journey. I know now that I did not lose them. I realize they are more bountiful than they have ever been. I was given a heart of kindness on this journey of a lifetime.

"One isn't necessarily born with courage, but one is born with potential. Without courage, we cannot practice any other virtue with consistency. We can't be kind, true, merciful, generous, or honest."
—Maya Angelou

"From Hope to Despair" to "A Journey of a Lifetime," Christopher's journey with his family, and "A Heart of Kindness"—thank you, everyone, for your kindness and life lessons. There is always gratitude for the kindest people with the kindest hearts. Thank you for helping me realize I still have my gifts and blessings.

With a Heart of Kindness,
Wendy Bernadette Comeau

Wendy Comeau

"We shall never know all the good that
a simple smile can do."
—Mother Teresa

Christopher & Wendy

"At times, our own light goes out and is rekindled
by a spark from another person. Each of us has cause to
think with deep gratitude of those who have lighted the flame
within us."
—Albert Schweitzer

I Have Room Left in My Heart

I can tell you that I have room left in my heart for the kind.
I have room left in my heart for the struggling.
I have room left in my heart for forgiveness.
I have room left in my heart for faith, hope, and charity.
I have room left in my heart for love and peace.
I have room left in my heart for strength and courage.
I have room left in my heart for understanding, sharing,
and caring.
I have learned there is no room left for anger in my heart.
There is no room left in my heart for people's judgment.
There is no room left in my heart for the self-centred.
There is no room left in my heart for the harsh words of
the unkind.
I have come to understand that our life and time is precious;
we do not get to choose how much time we have with the
people we love.
We do get the choice of how we are going to live our life.
We get the choice to value the time and life we have.

We get to make a difference in what we carry in our hearts. I am choosing to carry "A Heart of Kindness" because that is the legacy I was left when each one of my family members' hearts stopped beating.

They left me with A Heart of Kindness.

—Wendy Bernadette Comeau

"If you don't know about pain and trouble, you're in sad shape.
They make you appreciate life."
—Evel Knievel

Wendy Comeau

"A good book has no ending."
—R.D. Cumming

"Quality is not an act, it is a habit."
—Aristotle

References

Close, Glenn & Stuart, Heather (June 12, 2013). Overcoming mental illness means overcoming stigma. The *Globe and Mail*. https://www.theglobeandmail.com/opinion/overcoming-mental-illness-means-overcoming-stigma/article12480148/?arc404=true

Comeau-D'Orsay, Christopher "Good Morning."

Comeau-D'Orsay, Christopher "Forgive Me."

Comeau-D'Orsay, Christopher "In My life, I Think I Should Pray."

Comeau-D'Orsay, Christopher "The Cricket and the Spider."

Comeau, Wendy Bernadette "I Have Room Left in My Heart"

Davidovich Ockuly, Marta "When We Plant a Seed" (2017). Joy of Quotes. http://www.joyofquotes.com

Most widely spoken languages in the world. Infoplease.com https://www.infoplease.com/arts-entertainment/writing-and-language/most-widely-spoken-languages-world ("Most widely spoken languages in the word," n.d.).

National Institute of Neurological Disorders and Strokes (2017). http://www.ninds.nih.gov/Disorders/Patient-Caregiver-Education/Fact-Sheets/Batten-Disease-Fact-

Ombudsman Ontario (September 1, 2005). Drug funding: from hope to despair. Ombudsman Report. https://www.

ombudsman.on.ca/Investigations/SORT-Investigations/
Completed/Drug-funding---em-From-Hope-to-Despair--em-.
aspx

Ombudsman Ontario (June 22, 2006). The right to be impatient. 2005-2006 Annual Report. https://www.ombudsman.on.ca/Resources/Reports/2005-2006-Annual-Report. aspx#The_Right_To_Be_Impatient

Powers, Margaret Fishback. "Footprints."

Search Quotes. http://www.searchquotes.com (unknown). "Be sure to taste your words before you spit them out"

Wendy Comeau

CPSIA information can be obtained
at www.ICGtesting.com
Printed in the USA
LVHW01s0606130218
566367LV00024B/582/P